HOW TO SURVIVE IN COLLEGE

by Denny Rydberg

Zondervan Publishing House
Grand Rapids, Michigan

How to survive in college
Copyright © 1989 by Denny Rydberg

Published by the Zondervan Publishing House
1415 Lake Drive, S.E., Grand Rapids, Michigan 49506

Library of Congress Cataloging-in-Publication Data

Rydberg, Denny
    How to survive in college / by Denny Rydberg
    p. cm.
    "Youth books."
    ISBN 0-310-35351-3
    1. College student orientation—United States. 2. Study,
Method of. 3. College students—United States—Conduct of life.
I. Title.
    Lb2343.32.R93   1989
    307.1'4'0951—dc19   89–30748
                                                CIP

All Scripture quotations, unless otherwise noted, are taken from the
Holy Bible: New International Version (North American Edition).
Copyright © 1973, 1978, 1984 by the International Bible Society.
Used by permission of Zondervan Bible Publishers.

Edited by David Lambert and Lori Walburg

Illustration and Design by The Church Art Works, Salem, Oregon

Printed in the United States of America

89 90 91 92 93 94 / LP / 10 9 8 7 6 5 4 3 2 1

Dedication

To my dad and mom, whose love and support enabled me to survive college and beyond.

Acknowledgements

Thanks to my family: Marilyn, Heather, Josh, Jeremy and Jonathan, who always sacrifice when I write. Thanks to those twenty-two special contributors who have made a mark on this book. Thanks to the hundreds of college students who have taught me so much about survival and more. And thanks to Dave Lambert and my friends at Zondervan.

C O N T

ENTS

Part III. Extracurricular Life

SECTION

1

THE BASICS

CHAPTER

1

GOOD AND HARD
A Time of Discovery

College ain't easy.

A grammarian might take issue with that sentence. But it's the truth. College is difficult—more difficult than high school. The adjustments are more numerous, the temptations more fierce, the competition more keen, the course load more strenuous, the demands more than you've ever faced before. And usually you face all these pressures without as strong a support system as you had in high school.

Let me illustrate. Life to me is much like a race. Now, obviously, that analogy isn't new. The Apostle Paul talked about the Christian life as a race, and other writers have done the same. But the point I want to make is that the race of life is not a sprint. It's a marathon—a marathon run in sections.

If you're a recent high-school graduate reading this book, you've been running the race the last few years in a fairly familiar place, in your hometown and at your local high school. Family and friends have been watching. Some members of the community or neighborhood have known you. Teachers have called you by name. Friends from childhood have run the race with you. You may have been a member of a Young Life or Campus Life club, or part of a church youth group. Your network of support has been well established.

But now the race changes. Suddenly you're snatched from the familiar streets where you're known and you find yourself up on a road that circles the backside of the mountain, a mountain where people neither know you or care much about you. The road has twists and turns, numerous side roads, and steep hills. What makes this road even more difficult is that family, friends, classmates, and teachers are not lining the road, rooting you on, giving you oranges, Gatorade, and pats of encouragement.

But this mountainside road does have its advantages. The view sometimes is spectacular, and you gain a greater sense of independence and confidence as you run. You also get in better shape for the rest of the race as you carve your way up the road. You have more options, and that's intriguing. You have the freedom to run with abandon. And you have the freedom to fail. You can run or rest. Or, if you so choose, you may fall off the mountain. The network is not there monitoring your steps, pushing you on, giving you aid.

When I talk to high-school students on their way to college, I like to inform them of the new freedoms they'll discover. I tell them that they have the freedom never to go to sleep again, because no one will tell them what time to go to bed. They can stay out all night, every night, if they so desire. And no one will tell them what time to get up. If they don't want to, they will never have to get out of bed again. That's their choice.

College students can also skip all the classes they want (until grades come out!). No faculty member will call in midmorning and say, "All 750 of us are down here at Kane Hall, but I noticed you weren't here, and I wondered when you'd arrive so we could start. We certainly don't want you to miss anything."

I also tell high-school students, "If you go to

college, you'll never have to clean your room again!" I visit students in their residence halls and lead Bible studies in dorms and fraternities, and I've been in some rooms that smelled like a pair of used tennis shoes. Once the smell in the room was so bad that we in the group moved to another room. But that room was no better—it smelled like a sour washcloth! I've been in other college rooms over the course of a year and watched the dust visibly accumulate as time marched on. As the year progressed, the dust build-up reached astronomical proportions. The dust hill on the stereo became a mountain that by springtime created its own weather conditions! College students may not be sanitary, but they do know how to exercise their freedom not to clean.

Of course there are other freedoms in college. You can take drugs, experiment with alternative lifestyles, go wild. Or you can use the freedom to learn good discipline habits, develop long-lasting friendships, prepare for the future, strengthen yourself and others, and make a difference in the world. Those are the options at this stage of the race.

College allows you to explore the options, to discover for yourself some key truths about life and living. I asked some friends of mine who are recent college graduates to tell me what they discovered in college. Here are a few of their answers.

1. *"There is life outside*

the Wenatchee Valley." My friend Rod Handley gave me this one. You've probably never heard of the Wenatchee Valley, a rich farming area in eastern Washington State. But to Rod, who grew up in Wenatchee, the Valley was the center of the universe. Rod says, "I could not imagine anyone living, growing up, or retiring in any place but Wenatchee. But in college I discovered there were some people in this world who had never been to Wenatchee, and worse—there were some people who did not even know how to pronounce it."

Unlike Rod, I didn't grow up in Wenatchee, although I do know how to pronounce it. I grew up in a small town called Anacortes (also tough for some to pronounce), and I felt the same way that Rod did about Wenatchee. And when I got to college, I met other students who were just as proud and self-centered about their hometowns or home cities. Urban students were as provincial as those of us from the small towns. They thought their city was the cultural center of the world and any of us from small towns or other cities were definitely deprived individuals.

The point is that life is bigger than what you've known. And college helps you discover that fact.

2. *"My parents got a whole lot smarter while I was away at college."* Many of us are happy to move on to college for two reasons: (1) we're looking forward to being on our own and (2) we're looking forward to finally getting out of the house and away from our parents. As one of my friends noted: "During my last years of high school, I rarely sought out my parents' advice because I thought they wouldn't have any good input on my decisions. They were out-of-date and out of touch. But after arriving at college and being on my own, I realized my parents did have insights and were quality people. I appreciated them much more."

This is not a discovery you work at; it just happens. Parents naturally seem much more intelligent after you've been away for a while.

3. *"I had to prove myself all over again."* "My past reputation, my family, my community involvement meant absolutely nothing. I was accepted or rejected based on who I was."

After moving to a new place, almost everyone has to start from square one, and in some cases that's good. If you've been unproductive in high school or have had a reputation that wasn't too positive (whether it was deserved or not), you get a fresh start. For those who were stars in high school, starting over may be difficult. But it must be done. There's no way to get around it.

4. *"Seventy-five percent of what I learned at college did not come from my classes."* Doug Early, a graduate of the University of Washington who spent a year teaching English in China, gave me this one. He says, "Much of what I learned in college was about making it on my own: budgeting time, choosing priorities, and dealing with bureaucracy. I discovered in the process why employers place so much emphasis on a college degree. I think it's because they know that college graduates have successfully spent four or five years working in difficult situations to achieve a goal."

You can learn a lot about yourself, others, and life in general through your living situation—how to deal with messy roommate habits, or how to advise and encourage each other. You can learn from athletics, from student government, or even from the pressure of studying. Cramming, all-nighters, failing courses may be shocking as well as learning experiences.

Tim Hansel, an author, speaker, and friend, speaks of experiences as keys on a keychain. Each experience is another key that you can use to unlock a door in the future. You may not know where that door is yet. But later that key will be invaluable in opening a door that enables you to move into a new area of life.

I know from experience that God doesn't waste any experiences. He used my journalism in high school and college when I, almost by accident, became editor of a fledgling magazine. He used my time as both a starter and a substitute coming off the bench in basketball to allow me to identify with both the stars and the bench warmers. He used my successes and failures in relationships to give me insights about myself and to help me later in the counseling I do with students and adults. And he'll use all your experiences as well.

So collect some experiences. Reflect on them. Profit by them. College is a great way to spend four years or more getting an education, and much of that education has little to do with the classroom.

5. *"The process of getting both an education and a degree is a game that must be learned and played to* *succeed."* Mark Preslar is someone who learned to play the college game well. Having graduated from Arizona State University several years ago, he is now working on his Ph.D. in Soviet Studies. Here's what he says: "College is a game that can be either extremely fun and rewarding, or frustrating and very difficult. It is a game whose outcome will affect the rest of a person's life. Like any other game, college has objectives to be pursued and rules to be followed. Not clearly understanding the objectives and rules can put one at a serious disadvantage.

"Almost all careers require a person to fit within some particular hierarchy, some particular system, to play by that system's rules. One must successfully organize and plan, meet deadlines, interact with colleagues, be both under authority and in authority, learn to focus one's interests, and be in control of one's time and life. Playing the game in school, following the rules, interacting with professors and students, and getting good grades are all important parts of one's education."

Wise words from one who's played the game well—so well that he still plays it in graduate school.

6. *"I had to choose my friends and my lifestyle deliberately."* You may have grown up in a family that was always the first to arrive at church. You may have been from a home where you had no choice about showing up for classes, since you had to be on your deathbed before Mom let you miss school. You befriended certain people because your parents knew their families. You hung out with certain kids because they had been your peers for years.

College changes all that. Decisions are yours—

you choose who you'll hang out with and when you'll go to church or to class. Rod Handley writes, "Initially, the freedom was overwhelming; I found myself choosing friends and a lifestyle far different than what I'd experienced before. All of a sudden I found myself degenerating because I was not making the right decisions. I tried to hide things from people (especially my parents and close friends). But it did not take long to realize the freedom I had was causing me misery."

Many students have experienced in their first few months of college what Rod has described. The freedom is overwhelming; the temptations great. If you want quality people who can make a contribution to your life and you to theirs, you're going to have to make the choice to find those people and to spend time with them.

You're going to have to choose your lifestyle. And believe me, that will be tough. The lowest common denominator can easily prevail; people naturally tend to sink, not rise. College students with freedom on their hands can find a multitude of lifestyle options, many of them harmful, so fighting against a downward trend will take some conscious choices on your behalf.

And one last word on this subject. It's easier to start right than to start wrong and attempt some midcourse corrections. It's more effective to get off on the right foot than to trip, stumble, and fall, and then try to get up and move on. It's never too late to begin a comeback, and colleges are full of comeback stories, but a better use of time and energy is to consciously choose what friendships and lifestyle you want to pursue, and then move forward in those areas vigorously and *immediately.*

7. *"I learned a whole lot about finances!"* This is a reaction from a typical student. "In college, I had some freedom with my expenditures, and soon I discovered how precious money was and how quickly it could slip through my fingers. With little accountability, I had to begin to budget on my own and make a plan for earning, spending, and saving money. Budgeting was difficult at first, but it helped me prepare for the future."

Like all college students, when I was in college, I was always in financial need. I signed almost all my letters home, "Your son in abject poverty." Sometimes my pleas worked and I'd get a shekel or two in the mail. But looking back, I see that one of the major lessons I learned at college is one I'd heard but never experienced before: "There's no such thing as a free lunch." Because of that fact, I had to sacrifice some playtime for worktime. I had to take some part-time jobs even though that wasn't what I wanted most to do. But aside from limited scholarship money and some assistance on the part of my parents, I paid my way through college. So I felt a certain sense of satisfaction when I graduated, a feeling that I had "worked my way through." And, by the way, some of the best experiences I collected (see point 4, above) were at my jobs.

With the significant costs of college today, it's difficult for most students to pay their own way. Parental help and student loans provide a major chunk of tuition. But most of the students I know work part-time, either during the school year or in the summer or both. Working, budgeting, and assessing priorities are significant lessons learned from the money crunch.

8. *"My body wasn't ready for college."* College is a shock to the system. Most students don't get their eight hours of sleep, well-balanced meals, or regular exercise. Everything your high-school health education teacher preached and your parents reinforced is now up to you to accomplish. I know people who have been sick for weeks during the first quarter or semester of school because they never went to sleep before midnight, because they majored on fatty foods, and because they became couch potatoes.

Again, maintaining your physical health is up to you. You have to choose to exercise, choose to sleep (if your roommate will let you), and choose to forget the nightly run for pizza. Health choices are just another set of the multitude of choices you must make.

After looking over these eight points, we need to be realistic. Obviously, there are reasons college is tough. But there are also reasons college can be one of the best times of your life.

In the next chapters we'll explore what we've briefly touched on here, and we'll look at a great deal more. The purpose of this book is to enable you to survive college so that in four or five years you will emerge in great shape for the rest of life's race.

CHAPTER

2

DO YOU STILL HAVE A CHOICE?
A Dilemma

Which college is the right school for you? I have the answer! Are you ready? The answer is: *There is no one right school for you.* Contrary to popular opinion, there is no one "best school." Now that answer may seem disappointing. But it shouldn't be. The good news is that there are probably several dozen schools that could meet your needs and provide you with the opportunity for a quality, well-rounded education both inside and outside the classroom.

At this point, you may not care what the answer is. You feel the question is being asked after the fact. You've spent a couple of years already at a particular school and transferring would be out of the question. If you feel that way, skip this chapter.

However — don't skip it too quickly. If you're attending a college that doesn't meet your needs, if you're pretty sure you made a poor choice of schools, you may want to read on. You may even want to reconsider the transfer issue. It's one thing to be at a college that is not meeting your needs for two years; it's another to stay at that school for four! Two years could be considered a "learning experience," but four years is cruel and unusual punishment. Maybe it's time for you to move on. As a college pastor, I've met dozens of students who have transferred. They may lose some credits, they may gamble and find that the new school is not much better than the first, but at least they tried.

My wife was a transfer student. We both started at the same college, but in her sophomore year, under some financial pressure, she transferred from a Christian liberal arts college to a state university. She doesn't regret the move but appreciates what she gained from the Christian campus, and values what she learned at the University of Oregon. She sees the benefits of having attended both.

I stayed for four years. There were times when I thought about transferring for one reason or another, and twice I almost did. But both times I stayed put. I value my four years but wonder if maybe I should have moved on.

The point is: Transferring is not all bad. Some students can be academic nomads and migrate from place to place (beach campuses in the spring, ski campuses in the winter, football powers in the fall), and that can get ridiculous. But the relatively serious students who want to get the most from their college education shouldn't feel trapped by a decision they made a year or two ago. They should feel free to transfer if they feel they would benefit from the move.

Now for those in a decision-making mode, let's take a look at how we can make the best possible decision regarding our college career.

Choosing a college may seem like a momentous decision. And it is. But many guidance counselors have a tendency to make it seem even more momentous than it should be. Yes, you will be spending four or more years of your life there. Yes, this stage of your life is very formative. Yes, some of your friends and contacts for the future will come from your college experience so you want to choose your location well. *But* your choice of college is not a life-or-death situation. You can relax some.

Your choice of a university will *impact* your future, but it won't *determine* it. If you go to Stanford, an Ivy League school, or another school with an outstanding reputation nationally or regionally, employers' heads will be turned slightly. People will be impressed. And chances are the graduates of a renowned university will be high achievers who will make waves in the world and you will know them and have greater access to them. But later in life, the world looks for *production*, not *pedigree*. Who you are and what you do count more than where you went to school. Don't believe that there are only fifteen top schools in the country and that if you don't get into one of them, you are destined to second-class citizenship the rest of your life. There are great professors and great students and great opportunities at *many* colleges and universities. And some of the most prestigious universities are acclaimed not so much for their undergraduate programs as for their research and graduate schools, so don't limit yourself as you look at schools for your undergraduate years.

Now with those preliminary ideas in mind, how do you choose a college that is a good fit for you?

First of all, I strongly recommend praying and committing this decision to the Lord. To me, prayer should be the normal first step in the decision-making process. Let the Lord know that you want to do his will and that you'd appreciate some guidance in this area. He promises in his Word to give you what you need, and you need help in this choice. You probably won't get a supernatural answer; he probably won't speak to you in a dream and say, "Go to the University of Miami." But I'm confident God will speak through the decision-making process, helping you sense the answer through rational thoughts, advisors, campus visits, and gut feelings. Let God know that you want to do his bidding even when it comes to the choice of a university, for no matter what school you choose, he will go with you there, and he will use that school in your life.

I asked a good friend, Mark Hogendobler, a graduate of Princeton University in 1987 and now a Young Life staff member, to brainstorm with me on some questions to ask and steps to take as you consider a school. Here are some of the questions and suggestions that we compiled to help students, like you, who are going through the college selection process.

1. *What are your top priorities in a school?* Other ways of asking this question might be: What are your goals for the next four years? What do you want to get out of the college you attend? What do you want to accomplish by the end of your college career?

Mark decided that he wanted the best academic education possible. To him at that stage in his life, everything else was secondary. By secondary, Mark meant *everything*, including the location of the school, the kind of people there, the Christian fellowship, and the monetary sacrifice. But looking back on his decision he says, "I innocently assumed that I would be satisfied with the best education the United States had to offer. That was untrue. I could have compromised some on the quality of the program and gained tremendously in the social, interpersonal, and spiritual aspects of college." In other words, Mark wishes now that he had looked at other factors besides "best academic education."

Here are some other questions that help answer question 1.

2. *Do you want to go to a Christian university?* Christian colleges offer many advantages: Christian professors who want to help you develop a Christian worldview, a curriculum that is integrated with Christian beliefs, built-in fellowship opportunities, outstanding Christian speakers who visit the campus and speak at chapel, a chance to develop lifelong Christian friendships, and opportunities for Christian service.

But a Christian college also has its disadvantages. Sometimes apathy can stifle a campus where students take their Christianity for granted. Sometimes living in a cloistered environment where your faith isn't tested generates cynicism; free from outside attack, you may cynically chip away at your beliefs from the inside.

Larger state schools have their advantages and disadvantages as well. Advantages include having more options to choose from academically, having more money available for research, and having more of an opportunity to live out your faith in the face of opposition (you'll need the support of a Christian fellowship group to do this). The disadvantages are that you don't get to see how your faith integrates with academic "facts." You feel like Christianity is constantly under attack. And you have many distractions and temptations that might not be so obvious on a Christian campus. But usually a Christian fellowship group on a secular campus is alive and vibrant because it has to be. You are on the battlefield every day, and you can see the results of your faith and your prayers.

As a pastor who spends most of his time with students from a secular university and as an alumnus of a Christian university, I think I have a unique perspective. I appreciate what I received from my education. I am thankful for professors who took an interest in me and grateful for the academic excellence and Christian character of my alma mater. But I also see the tremendous advantages for Christians living out their faith in a secular environment. The fellowship in the college group where I minister now is more alive than anything I saw at my Christian alma mater. However, I also see more disasters on our campus now than I did in college as I watch both Christians and non-Christians alike succumb to pressures and temptations.

From my experience, I recommend that you not make a quick decision on the Christian college issue but carefully consider other factors as well. A Christian school may not automatically be the best for you. On the other hand, a large state school may not best fit your needs.

3. *What about the* **type** *and* **size** *of the school?* Do you prefer a large school or a small one? You might want to talk to others about the advantages of each. A large school, for instance, provides more options, but it can also seem very cold and impersonal. You can get lost in the crowd—but maybe that's what you want. A small school usually has less options and more personal involvement. Whether the school is large or small, you can probably make a place for yourself at either.

My co-worker Carolyn Duffy recommends large universities from experience: "I was always told, before going to a campus with 34,000 students, that I'd never see the same face twice and that a smaller school would be so much better for me academically and socially. People also told me that in a big school I'd be just another number. But I chose to go to the large state university anyway, anticipating the great challenge of finding my niche and seeing how it all worked together. I loved every minute of it and have never wished I'd made a decision for a smaller state or private school."

Mark Hogendobler, however, disagrees with Carolyn: "I say small school all the way, but I've found that most people know what they like—whether a big school or a small one—and no number of pros and cons will really change their mind. And if they do change their mind, they may very well end up unhappy because their natural bent is for the other kind of school."

Besides considering school size, you also need to consider school type. Do you want a public or private school? Do you want a strongly liberal arts school, which will give you a well-rounded education, or a school that emphasizes specialized programs in the sciences? As you can see, what *type* of school you need to fit your talents and interests is just as important to decide as what *size* of school you are comfortable with.

4. *What major course of study will you pursue?* If you don't know the answer to this question, take comfort: Most people don't know what their major is when they begin college, and even if they do, that major will often change. I came into college wanting to major in psychology and prepare for medical school. Medical school went out the window early, but I continued in psychology. Most people switch majors before they're through with college, but if you're decided on what you'd like to study, look at schools that are strong in that area. If oceanography is your thing, you'll probably not want to go to a landlocked university. Or if you love English, you won't want a school that specializes in chemical engineering and gives only moderate support to the English department.

5. *Do you want to find a school that will serve as a springboard to graduate school?* In other words, are you looking for a college that will give you the best opportunity to get into a specific medical school or law school or other graduate school? If so, you would want to look at the graduate schools first, determine what qualifications they desire and what undergraduate schools they value, then make your decision based on graduate schools first and undergraduate schools second.

6. *What's the student/faculty ratio—the number of students compared to the number of faculty?* Usually the fewer students to professors is a good indication that you'll get more personalized attention. Check out that ratio both within the school in general and within the department of your major. In addition, find out how much money the school spends on that department compared to other departments and schools.

7. *Is it important for you to be with friends from high school?* If so, where do most of them attend?

8. *Is location a prime consideration?* Do you want to be close to home to keep up with friends and family, or do you want to make the break and see how you can survive on your own? Does a particular area of the country intrigue you and invite you to explore it further? Do you prefer living in the city or in the country, in the sun or in the snow, in the mountains or in the flatlands? Do you prefer the East, the Midwest, the South, or the West Coast? Remember, the types of people you meet and the things you do in your free time will depend for a large part on what town or city you decide to study in.

9. *Are sports important to you?* Sports, both intercollegiate competition and intramurals, are a big part of the college experience. You may want a school where you can start, or a school where you can play, or just a school where you can watch your favorite game. Maybe you like the traditional fall football days, when together with ninety thousand other fans you enjoy the crisp autumn weather as you cheer your team to victory. Or maybe you like the friendly competition of intramural sports. If so, does the administration encourage intramural athletics for both sexes? Is the organization and administration of the program solid and consistent over the years? If a particular kind of sport is important to you, you will want to make sure that the school you choose offers the facilities and teams for that sport.

10. *What about other extracurricular activities?*

What else interests you? Does the school offer it? Can you try out for a part in a school play, for instance, or do you have to be a drama major to apply? Is there a mountaineering group, an organization for jugglers, a clown troupe, an astronomy society, a club for parachutists? Check it out.

11. *Is there a special professor whose books you admire and with whom you'd like to study?* You may choose a college simply in order to study under someone you admire. Part of college life is finding mentors in your chosen profession, people who will help you discover and develop your own gifts even as their example inspires you. However, before you make a decision to attend a college just to have a certain professor, make sure that you will be able to take courses from him or her. Some well-known professors, for instance, only teach graduate courses.

12. *Do you want to be near a certain church?* Perhaps you would like to go to school to be near a certain pastor or church whose ministry you admire. But don't pin your hopes and decision on one person, whether that person be a professor or a pastor. People move on, and they don't always ask your permission to do so.

13. *What are the opportunities for Christian fellowship and ministry?* You will spend at least four years of your life at the college of your choice, and that's a long time to go without fellowship. You'll need the support of the Christian community, so be sure you have access to one. Also check into ministry opportunities in the area, such as Young Life groups, Campus Life groups, and church groups. Obviously, you can develop fellowship groups and ministry opportunities anywhere, but having these available when you arrive on campus is a great advantage.

14. *What about the living situation?* What is the percentage of students who live on campus? Usually the more students that live on campus, the more you will feel the "college atmosphere." If everyone commutes, the flavor is much different than if students live on campus. Is there room for students who want to live on campus or is there a long waiting list? If you have to live off campus, what are the options? Are the apartments attractive or will you have to live in a dump? Do you want to be in a fraternity or sorority? What's the Greek system like? Respected? Degraded? Will you need a car or is the public transportation adequate? Keep in mind that you won't want to feel trapped at school. You'll want to get away at times, so transportation is a definite issue.

15. *Have you visited the school?* One trip to the school can tell you subtle things that all the informational brochures and statistics could never depict. While you're at the school, you have the opportunity to check out the facilities of everything that interests you, from chemistry labs to tennis courts, from residence halls to nearby movie theaters. You can eat in the commons and attend a few classes. If the school provides you with a "guide," don't spend all your time with him or her. Be bold—ask students at random how they feel about the school. Make a list of questions in advance and get as many answers as you can. Talk to folks who are majoring in the field you are interested in. How do they view the school?

16. *Have you talked to alumni from the school?* Alumni can offer some valuable insights on the college and what kind of experience you are likely to have there. Of course, you will need to assess their comments according to how they contrast or compare to you. For example, if someone recommends a college because he had a great time attending all the football games, and football happens to bore you to tears, the advice of that alumnus will naturally carry less weight. But if the former editor of the school newspaper recommends it to you as a place to get the journalism experience you desire, take her opinions seriously.

17. *What about your financial resources and the costs of the school?* My father-in-law often says, "The quality is long remembered after the price is forgotten." That's good advice for storm windows (which he sells) as well as for college. You'll remember the quality of your education and your experience long after you've paid the last of your college loans. But you need to be wise in this area as well (and your parents will probably see to it that you are!). How much can you spend? Or, a better question, how much have you already saved for your college education?

How much can your parents afford? Are you willing to take out a student loan? What scholarship opportunities exist?

Speaking of scholarships, don't just look at scholarships that originate from the school you're attending. Go to your school guidance counselor and check out all the scholarships that exist. There are many ways to fund an education but you have to dig for them. People are paid to help you in this area so check out your high school or college guidance office. Fraternal orders (like the Elks and Eagles), service clubs, some corporations, and individual donors make scholarships available to needy or deserving students.

In considering finances, note that some schools that have a more expensive total expense figure can actually end up being less expensive because these schools have more scholarship money to invest in their students. Princeton is an ideal example. It promises that anybody who is granted admission will be able to afford to go. A great policy, don't you think?

18. *Are you satisfied with your research?* You can't be satisfied with your research until you do some, so research, research, research. Schools love to send information—that's why their admissions departments exist. Except for your stamp, the information is free. Right now you're in a "buyer's market." Most universities are competing for students. They want to help you make your decision; they want to inform and inspire you. Let them.

Remember: It's better to over-aim than under-aim. Don't underestimate yourself. Try to get into the college that meets most of your priorities even if you think, "They'd never take me" or "It's too expensive."

And don't be afraid to transfer. I've known students who chose to attend a state university near their home because they were afraid to move away. But now that they are a year or two older they may be able to take the step they feared upon graduation.

Finally, as my friend Doug Early advises, "Be willing to risk. Listen to your instincts about a college." In other words, listen to your feelings. I know real estate salespeople who say that you can tell in the customers' eyes when they have found "their home." When you're choosing a college, you're looking for a life as well as a home. So don't go totally on the intellect or the rational to make your decision. Listen to your *feelings* about a college as well.

Remember that there will always be a few regrets wherever you go. One school won't provide all you need or want, and you may even decide that college isn't for you. But with prayer and some careful thought, you'll make the choice that's right for you.

Do You Still Have a Choice?

CHAPTER

3

SPIRITUAL SURVIVAL
First Things First

When I give advice on how to survive college, I could address many topics. How to study is a biggie, and specifically how to study in specialized areas like the humanities, the sciences, or the arts. In the social arena we need help with developing new friendships and getting along with people. Personally, we need encouragement in the face of disappointments. Practically, we need advice on how to handle a part-time job and still be a good student. And finally, we may be concerned with how to make a difference in our campus and the world while still pursuing a college education. All these topics are important, and this book will examine them.

But the most important topic of all is how to survive spiritually—how to keep your relationship with the Lord fresh and alive. If you do everything else well, graduate summa cum laude, are elected President of the Student Body by the widest margin of victory in the history of the institution, make consensus All American in your chosen sport, fall in love with the most attractive person on campus (next to you, of course), and surprise everyone by becoming a multimillionaire in your part-time job—but don't survive spiritually, you'll feel empty inside.

Jesus certainly put spiritual well-being first. He said, "Seek first his kingdom and his righteousness, and all these things will be given to you as well" (Matt. 6:33). What are "all these things"? Your food, your clothes, your money—everything else you need, in fact.

But as I write these words, I want you to know

from the beginning that I am not Peter Piety. I have not walked with God closely every moment of my life. I grew up in a Christian home, made a commitment to Jesus Christ at an early age, was involved in leadership with youth groups and beyond. But there have been times in my life, I'm sad to say, when I didn't walk closely with the Lord. And I paid for it. Through those disobedient times, I've learned that spiritual survival is a must, that you can have a lot of success on the outside, but if your spiritual tank is empty on the inside, you're hurting yourself immensely and you're setting yourself up for some major disappointments and disasters.

The Importance of Spiritual Survival

You can't turn your back on God and expect to emerge unscathed. It's not that he's some great policeman or vice-principal in the sky who hits you with his stick when you do wrong. It's just that he's established some cause and effect relationships. The Bible says you reap what you sow: When you walk with God, you reap his direction, his peace, his purpose; you sense that life has meaning and that you're part of what he has in mind. When you choose to walk away from God either in an overtly rebellious or quietly passive manner, you reap the consequences of being out-of-touch with the Creator of the universe and the Lord of your life. It's that simple. And, frankly, being out of touch is dangerous. The further you move from God, the more trouble can come into your life. Little steps of disobedience lead to bigger steps of disobedience. The individual actions become bad habits and the bad habits become obsessions and compulsions that are very difficult to escape.

Let me give you an example. I have a good friend who is a success. He's been a major star in athletics, particularly in tennis. He was captain of his university team for two years in a major university with a very competitive program. He was ranked number one on the team and won some big tournaments. He did well in school, served on one of the university's most prestigious committees, and upon graduation received a good job offer with an investment firm.

But early in his college years, he strayed in one area of his life. Although a Christian, he chose to ignore God's warnings about premarital sex and got involved physically with his girlfriend, also a Christian. He put that relationship and that desire above his desire to walk with God. Over the months, the sexual relationship became almost obsessive and inflicted scars that my friend and his former girlfriend are still facing. He has returned to obedience, but the scars remain and the healing is still in process. My own experience and the experience of my friend tell me that our spiritual life, our relationship with Christ, our obedience to his words, and our very spiritual survival should be paramount in our thoughts and priorities.

As a friend and pastor of college students, I've watched wonderful people get casual in their

relationship with the Lord and begin to drift—slowly at first and then more quickly—and the results have been saddening to me and I'm sure to God. When God created us, he knew what would be best for us. He provided us with some instructions in his Word, the Bible, but even more, he provided us with a relationship with him and through him with other believers. These instructions and these relationships were designed to help us survive and succeed in this world. His laws were not designed to hamper us or hinder us but to help us. God desires to free us to be all that we can be, to enable us to live life with a minimum of regrets and a maximum of joy. By telling us to seek first his kingdom and his righteousness, he lets us know that he wants the best for us.

When we have our relationship with God as our top priority, we are prepared to face everything that life throws at us, including the college experience.

Not only is spiritual survival stressed so early in this book because it's the most *important* aspect of life, but also because when you enter college there is a sense of *urgency*.

The time is urgent because when you enter college, you enter with the freedom to choose whether or not to take God along. Some of us use our newfound freedom to go on vacation from God. We're not deliberately rebellious. Sometimes we don't even intend the vacation—it "just happens." Mom and Dad aren't there to "encourage" us to go to church. Our youth leader isn't calling all the time. Our buddies from church or Young Life or Campus Life aren't there, we have greater anonymity, people don't know our past, no one is particularly fired up about Christianity, and it's suddenly easy to take it easy, to drift.

I personally believe that the first six weeks of a person's college career are crucial in establishing patterns and relationships with family, friends, and the Lord. Within the first six weeks of college, freshmen or transfer students make numerous decisions about the kind of people they want to hang out with for the next few years and about the lifestyle they want to live. They establish patterns that will be difficult to break from later.

To help students set a good pattern early in the semester, my ministry at the University of Washington is organized and ready to minister as soon as classes begin. We don't want to wait for students to come to us in order to start anything. Instead, we want Bible studies organized, small groups begun, publicity out. We want to let students know that we have an attractive, vibrant fellowship going and that we'd love for them to be involved. Our staff knows that it's easier for students to make right choices at the beginning than it is for them to change later. Granted, comebacks occur, and we encourage students to make a spiritual comeback regardless of where they've been. People can later change friends and a lifestyle they regret, but it is far more difficult to change later than to seek God and Christian fellowship first.

Besides importance and urgency there are also some practical reasons for wanting to make spiritual survival of utmost importance.

1. *Your identity is often molded by those with whom you spend the most time.* If you decide to ignore God and stay away from other believers who will encourage and challenge you, you will have to face some consequences. Without God's direction in your life and the encouragement and accountability of other Christian brothers and sisters, the opportunities for living life at a lesser spiritual and moral level are greater, and you will likely court disaster.

2. *All of us need direction.* To find direction, we need wisdom, God's wisdom, a wisdom far better than whatever other human beings alone can offer. As we walk with God, trust him, and acknowledge him as Lord of our lives, he leads us. The writer of Proverbs says, "Trust in the Lord with all your heart and lean not on your own understanding; in all your ways acknowledge him, and he will make your paths straight" (Proverbs 3:5-6). If we turn our backs on him, we lose that sense of leadership, and we lose access to his direction and wisdom in our lives.

In the New Testament, we read this promise. "If any of you lacks wisdom, he should ask God, who gives generously to all without finding fault, and it will be given him. But when he asks, he must believe and not doubt, because he who doubts is like a wave of the sea, blown and tossed by the wind. That man should not think he will receive anything from the Lord; he is a double-minded man, unstable in all he does" (James 1:5-8). College is a time when we make many major decisions. We choose a major, decide on a possible career, and sometimes find our marriage partner. With those kinds of decisions facing us, we need all the help we can get from the Lord. If we put him first, he will give us the wisdom to make these decisions.

3. *We need clarity and focus in our lives in the midst of all the pressures we feel.* So many people—

parents, peers, professors, and even ourselves—have expectations for our lives. It's liberating and clarifying to know that God wants the best for our lives, that he understands us perfectly, and that he doesn't make unrealistic demands or place unbelievable expectations on us. When we "play to an audience of One" instead of to many, when we realize that it is only God that we must ultimately please and that he knows us and doesn't demand more than we can handle, and when we simply attempt to do our best through his power in our lives, we are better able to deal with life. Some of the confusion is eliminated, as well as some of the pressure.

4. *Walking with Christ gives us joy and peace.* And those are two commodities in the world that are in short supply. The ability to be at peace and express joy in the midst of poor test scores, financial hardship and disappointing relationships, as well as when things are going well, is a testimony to the presence and work of Jesus Christ in our lives. Joy and peace are not traits that we can pro- duce on our own; they are by-products of a healthy relationship with God.

The college experience at times is mentally and emo- tionally exhausting. There are times when you want to give up or die—literally. Maybe you've been mismanaging time all term and now the end is near, putting you in deep trouble. Or you've been struggling since day one with a difficult subject and you haven't progressed much further than when you started. At those times anxiety often creeps in and kills whatever capacity you had for meaningful relationships or quality study time. You feel as if your goals are unrealistic and enormously beyond you. In the midst of these feelings, it is good to know that you are loved and cared for. It's comforting to know that you are incredibly valuable to the One who made this universe that you are studying.

God loves us more than we could ever understand. He is mindful of our struggles and sorrows, and he is conscious of our helplessness. Ask him to free you from the anxiety you feel and replace that with peace. Ask him to clear your mind and maximize your study times. He will.

5. *Walking with Christ gives us a community.* That community of men and women, the church, comprises the Body of Christ. As part of that body, we have support, support to overcome social pressures, to say no to the culture when we need to. In addition, because the friends we make in college usually are more enduring than the ones we've known in high school, this Christian community helps us develop some friendships that will last well into the future.

How to Survive Spiritually in College

With those practical advantages in front of us, how do we stay spiritually fit, spiritually fresh, spiritually alive? That's the big question. I've gathered some suggestions for spiritual survival from recent graduates, then added a few of my own. For the help of two of my good friends, Mike Gaffney and Rod Handley, I'm especially grateful, since they helped me compile the following points.

1. *You've got to want a relationship with God.* As Rod Handley says, "Unless you have the apostle Peter as your roommate and Paul as your best friend, God won't accidentally become a priority." You've got to *want* God, to *go* for him. If you don't have that hunger for the Lord, I suggest that your first prayer be, "Lord, give me a desire for you."

2. *Develop a personal quiet time.* In other words, discipline yourself each day to spend time with God, reading the Bible and praying. The quiet time doesn't have to be long or involved; you don't have to do the same thing every day. There are many books written on how to have a quiet time and many publications designed for use *in* a quiet time. Find the location of your nearest Christian bookstore, then check out their resources if you want. Meanwhile, to get you started, here are some guidelines for having a quiet time.

• *Have a regular time and a regular place.* It's easier to have some regularity than to try to find a new place and time for devotions each day. Try to choose a place that is relatively free from noise and distractions. This might be difficult if your dorm or house is an active place—you may have to have your quiet time in the library or get up earlier than the rest of your household does. And try to choose a time when you're not on the verge of falling asleep; being alert will make your quiet time that much better.

• *Read some Scriptures.* You may read a few verses, a chapter, or a section for a devotional reading. Do whatever you prefer, and plan to read a variety of

Spiritual Survival

things. Variety *is* the spice of life—even your devotional life—so if you get stagnant, change your approach.

- *Write down what you've learned.* Keep a notebook or journal where you write down what God has said to you that day. It doesn't have to be lengthy; it doesn't have to be profound. But it's fun and helpful to look back months later and see how God has consistently taught you from his Word.

- *Pray.* Thank God for who he is and for his blessings in your life. Pray for the world, for what you've learned in classes, for family, for friends—and even for yourself.

- *Remember that it is a great privilege to spend time with the Creator of the Universe, the Lord of all.* God is your friend and wants you to know him, so try to be "all there" when you're with him. Ask him to help you remove the distractions from your mind. Concentrate on him and what he wants to share with you. Think of this time as an "appointment with God," realizing that he calls you not only to love him, but also to fear him—to have awe, reverential trust, and a healthy respect for him.

3. *Pray throughout the day.* The apostle Paul called this kind of prayer, "praying without ceasing." I don't think that meant that he walked through life with his head down, eyes closed, talking out loud. Praying without ceasing means having a prayerful attitude as you move through the day. When you believe that God is your closest friend, that he loves you and wants you to express what's on your mind, you can feel free to fire off some quick prayers (some call them "bullet prayers") as you meet people, take a test, work on a paper, or see a need. Keep the communication lines open—pray often throughout the day.

4. *Confess sin and practice forgiveness.* Part of prayer is confession. We hinder communication with God when we sin and don't get rid of the guilt or bitterness accompanying that sin. Confession opens up the lines of communication and is good for the soul, giving us a clean slate, a fresh start. First John 1:9 says, "If we confess our sins, he is faithful and just and will forgive us our sins and purify us from all un-righteousness."

My senior pastor, Bruce Larson, refers to sin as "stepping on the hose." When we sin, we hinder the Holy Spirit's life-giving source much the same as we disrupt the flow of water when we step on a garden hose. Confession is getting off the hose and allowing love, faithfulness, and justice to forgive us, cleanse us, and empower us.

Confessing moment by moment is also important because harbored sin hardens us and takes us further away from God. In this case, we don't merely step on the hose but actually move away from it. God then cannot flow through us and cleanse us until we draw near and repent.

Not forgiving others is also a way to step on the hose. Throughout the Bible, the relationships of person-to-person and person-to-God are intertwined. Jesus says that if we are offering our gift at the altar (doing a religious act) and have something against another person, we need to take care of that relationship before we go back to the altar (Matthew 5:23). He knew that people conflicts affect our relationship with him. It's important to forgive others when they wrong us and to ask them for forgiveness when we wrong them so that the bitterness we feel in unresolved relationships doesn't cloud our relationship with Christ. We must be not only quick confessors, but also aggressive forgivers.

5. *Get involved in an ongoing fellowship.* It's not enough to have a personal relationship with Christ; you also need a corporate relationship. God puts us in families, he puts us in communities. So plug into a group somewhere. And take solace in the fact that wherever you go, there will be a fellowship group somewhere. You may have to look hard to find it, but God normally won't send you anywhere where there aren't a few other Christians around. Ask your pastor or youth leader before you leave for college if he or she knows of any good groups near your campus. Check out churches near the university, research some of the campus organizations like Inter Varsity, Campus Crusade, or your denomination's campus ministry.

Find the group, then go to it, introduce yourself, and ask questions. Decide fairly quickly whether this group is for you. And remember no group is perfect. Like a friend of mine said, "If the group was perfect, they wouldn't let you in." So get involved in spite of the small imperfections. Get so involved that people notice when you're not there. Then you'll remember how important you are to the group and how important they are to you. If you have problems being faithful to the group, ask someone to hold you accountable or to help you get there. You will be blessed by consistently going no matter how emotionally up or down you might feel on that particular meeting night.

6. *Get into a small group.* Your primary fellowship group may be moderate in size or quite large, so try to get involved in a more intimate, small-group situation. A small group is three to ten people who meet regularly and share honestly and openly with each other. Good small groups spend some time catching up on what happened in that week, doing Bible study, sharing needs, and praying for one another. A small group keeps us sharp and sane; Proverbs 27:17 says, "As iron sharpens iron, so one man sharpens another."

I've been in different small groups most of my life. My first was in my junior year of college when four or five guys gathered in my room for a quick time of check-in and a longer time of prayer. Because that group meant so much to me, I have sought out other small groups even after graduating from college.

A good place to have a small group is within your living situation. If there's not a small group of Christians already meeting, organize one, even if you're a freshman. Last spring, a frosh guy from one of the fraternities on our campus started up a Bible study in his house. I was honored to participate with them, and I saw over just five weeks how helpful that group was for the Christians in the house. They sharpened and strengthened one another. But someone needed to have the courage to put it together—and my friend Craig did.

7. *Worship.* Make sure you worship regularly, at least through your fellowship group. But I also recommend you worship on Sunday mornings with the wider family of God in a church. Sometimes in college, we get caught up in a "university ghetto," spending all our time with students. It's important to branch out, to attend a church where we can see that God works through generations of people, and to join with all generations in praising God.

8. *Persevere.* Life is a battle. The Bible says our primary adversary is the devil, Satan, the evil one. Peter understood spiritual battle well and says this: "Be self-controlled and alert. Your enemy the devil prowls around like a roaring lion looking for someone to devour. Resist him, standing firm in the faith, because you know that your brothers throughout the world are undergoing the same kind of sufferings" (1 Peter 5:8-9).

Not far from our home lives an animal trainer who keeps a lion, a tiger, and other wild animals on her property. She trains them for filming commercials and videos, and for making presentations to school assemblies and corporate groups. Once, while making an industrial film, one of the trainer's friends was attacked and seriously injured by Sultan, the tiger. Why? Because the woman tripped and fell, and when anyone is on the ground, the natural instincts of the cat take over; the person on the ground becomes "prey." The woman was bitten and dragged before the trainer and other helpers could free her.

Several years ago the trainer and her lion came to church to be part of my children's sermon. One of the questions I asked the trainer was, "Is the lion tame?" She answered, "He's trained but not tame. No wild animal is ever tame."

Like Sultan, Satan is not tame. He is well-trained in disruption and warfare. Like Sultan the tiger, he pounces on those who are down. And he boldly attacks us even while we're upright. But the apostle

John, who faced many spiritual battles in his life, gives us this good news about the battle: "You, dear children, are from God and have overcome them, because the one who is in you [the Spirit of Jesus Christ] is greater than the one who is in the world" (1 John 4:4). In other words, if we trust Christ and walk with him, we have the power to win. But we need to hang in there, because life can be tough; God didn't promise us a Disneyland or a rose garden—or an easy life.

One of the ways we can persevere when we're struggling against a certain sin is to find a trustworthy friend who can and will hold us accountable in that area. For example, suppose you are struggling with the sin of lust and have been feeding that desire with R-rated videos and soft-core pornographic reading. You've prayed about the problem but haven't been able to kick the habit, and now, after repeated failures, you feel overwhelmed and increasingly discouraged. I suggest you share your struggle with a trustworthy friend and ask him or her for help. What form does this help take? First your friend hears your struggle and your confession, then helps you develop a game plan for dealing with the problem (for instance, no more R-rated films, and no *Playboy*), then checks with you to make sure you're following the plan.

An accountability relationship works on other areas besides lust. I happened to choose lust because when I did a survey of college students, I found that number one on their list of temptations was lust. But accountability can work with eating disorders, a battle with self-image, procrastination, and many other problems.

I have several students who are in an accountability relationship with me. One couple has been struggling in the physical area of their relationship, so we sat down together and drew up a contract. They signed the contract and I have it in a "secret" file in my office labeled **FMEO**—*For My Eyes Only*. Part of the contract is that one of the two people calls me and tells me how the week went. I hold them accountable for their physical relationship with each other.

You may want to have a similar arrangement with a close friend as you seek to fight the good fight, to persevere in faith and righteousness.

9. *Be a seeker of truth.* Walk honestly and uprightly, keeping your word, living according to God's commands, and seeking truth diligently. Read your college books with a Christian filter, sorting out the true from the false. Then read some Christian books as well. And in the midst of all your reading, don't neglect the Bible, the best of all sources of truth.

10. *Share your faith.* This is a special and strategic time in your life. You have only four years of your life to be an insider on a college campus. For only four years can you be a member of a residence hall, athletic team, or some other student group. At the end of that time, you become an alumnus. You're no longer an insider. You don't live in that dorm or house any longer. You're not a member of that squad, that group. And all those students with whom you spent so much time are gone. Your window of opportunity to share the good news on a college campus as an insider is limited, so *this* is the time to make a difference where you are.

Remember, many of the students you know will later become leaders in their communities and the world. If you bring the good news to these students, someday they may bring Christ with them into their leadership positions.

Sharing your faith also encourages growth in your own life, sharpening your perception of who God is and giving you confidence as you see his power evidenced in your life. Witnessing is yet another way of staying spiritually fit.

11. *Take some leadership positions.* You can keep your relationship with Christ fresh by stepping outside of the old comfort zone and taking more responsibility in leadership. Perhaps you might act as leader of your living group, fellowship group, or church group. Or maybe you could put together a ministry that's never been done on campus before. You'll be amazed at what the Lord can do through you when you take a risk and make yourself available.

Finally, know that you're never in a place where God hasn't already been and already is. He doesn't leave us alone. But he does call us to be partners with him to maintain our own spiritual well-being. He wants us to put first things first—and that means keeping ourselves spiritually fit.

CHAPTER

4

THINKING "CHRISTIANLY"
*Developing a
Christian Worldview*

What does it mean to think "Christianly"? What does it mean to have a Christian worldview? And why do I as the author address this subject so early in a book on surviving college?

To think Christianly means that we don't compartmentalize our life, that we don't separate our daily life from our spiritual life. Rather, in everything we do, from playing athletics to relating to a houseful of students, from working out complex chemistry problems to studying Russian history, we work at seeing everything through God's eyes and from his viewpoint. We don't say, "Well, that's physics. Christianity is what I do on Tuesday night at my fellowship group." What we do as Christians consumes 100 percent of our time. In physics, we examine truth, but we bring our faith with us. We don't see a difference between faith and truth. God is a big God and can handle the formulas and data we discover.

To have a Christian worldview means that we try to see the world and historical events from God's perspective. It means that we have a set of values and beliefs that we use to operate in any circumstance. We are not into situational ethics. Instead, we strive for consistency, hoping to relate our faith to our studies and our actions.

There is a great difference between a Christian worldview and a secular one. Humanism, meditation, the New Age "visualization" of world peace, health and wealth doctrines are all counterfeits. Success in the world's view and success from a Christian's view differ. The world says there are no absolutes; everything is relative. But a Christian, even at the risk of being called closed-minded, says there *are* absolutes.

Christians believe in the absolute truth of Scripture, that God has revealed himself to us in his Word. We believe in God's absolute love for us as revealed in the sacrifice of his Son, Jesus Christ. And we believe in the absolute sin of humanity. In the Christian worldview, selflessness is emphasized rather than self-fulfillment; servanthood rather than power; and conforming to Christ rather than conforming to the world.

Patty Burgin has been working with students since she graduated from college. Here is what she says about her own personal pilgrimage and the development of her worldview.

"In the fall of 1968 I was a freshman. I thought of myself as moderately, appropriately, religious. That meant (1) a nostalgic attachment to church with the family at Christmas and Easter, and (2) fairly moral behavior in between. It had never occurred to me that anything of a radical or revolutionary nature would ever be associated with religion, because religion in 1968 was a comfortable presence, appropriate in its compartment. But in 1968 the world exploded for other students and for me.

"That was the year that America was starting to lose her way in Vietnam. The year had begun with a terrible defeat in Southeast Asia. That spring, Dr. Martin Luther King was assassinated, students at Columbia University seized their administration buildings, and a song and a movie about a student losing his idealism and innocence ("The Graduate") topped the charts. Two days before our high-school graduation, Bobby Kennedy was shot. Through the summer, the poor marched in Washington, Soviet tanks rolled into

Czechoslovakia, and there were battles in the streets of Chicago during the Democratic Convention. In the fall, Richard Nixon won reelection, Apollo 8 circled the moon, and the Beatles recorded their last album.

"Events helped to spawn and then nurture a philosophy of life that encouraged students to hold passionate convictions. But holding to moral absolutes about things like God, or our sexuality, we reasoned, only led to intolerance. And, we believed, intolerance was categorically wrong.

"Thus passionate convictions were supposed to fit with moral relativism. But they didn't. And like many of my peers, I spent much of my time the first two years in college failing to achieve that oxymoron, moral relativism. My personal response was to become a half-hippie, half-sorority woman environmental activist who, for comic relief, dated cowboys.

"By the fall of 1970, I had the 'blahs about the cause.' After seeing the 'movement' from the inside, I was upset by the short-sighted hypocrisy and moral mediocrity that marked much of what went on. The highest virtue was the ability to tolerate, even applaud, every conceivable philosophy of life.

"That fall I ran across the words of King Solomon in the book of Ecclesiastes. Life would be far easier, he suggested, had God not planted 'eternity in our hearts.' As soon as I had read the words, I knew they were true. I was not here by chance but by God's choice. I had been created with dignity and significance. Increasingly I wondered if truth and morality existed in an absolute form. Was there a God? Did he care? Did anything in the heritage I had so impetuously rejected have bearing on the answers?

"On October 17, 1970, I quietly and confidently gave my life to Jesus Christ.

"By the time I became a Christian, people were even attaching words like 'revolutionary' to walking with Jesus. But as we move toward the close of the millennium, students who yearn to feel deeply, to think clearly, and to live consistently find themselves fighting an opposing trend."

The opposing trend that Patty mentions is the trend to keep Jesus in his place, to moderate and compartmentalize his influence in our lives. The trend is to create an image of Jesus, says Patty, "that will bestow comfort, bless self-involved preferences, halt the need to suffer or sacrifice, and shrug benignly at morally mediocre choices." It is that trend that I'd like to see us fight.

How do we fight the trend? How do we go about thinking Christianly and developing a Christian worldview? Here are some suggestions on which Patty, Eric Lingren, a 1986 university graduate, and I collaborated.

1. *Pray.* Ask God to renew your mind, to help you think, to make your faith a part of your daily life. Ask God to help you see the world through his eyes. Focus your mind and heart on God, and he will guide you.

2. *Examine your assumptions.* What do you believe about God? What do you believe about yourself? If you are walking with Jesus Christ, directed and empowered by his Spirit, you are increasingly aware that "you are not your own" (1 Cor. 6:19), that every area of your life matters to him (Col. 3), and that his desire is for you to represent him with consistency and effectiveness both in what you do and in what you say (2 Cor. 5).

What are your views about relationships, money, politics, domestic and foreign affairs, religion, appearances, motives, integrity? What are the beliefs and values of others? How do your assumptions compare and contrast? In what ways do you need to align your views more with God's?

3. *Examine what you think and hear in the light of Scripture.* We are called to know Scripture (Psalm 119) and to test the ideas and beliefs and values we encounter (Acts 17:11). Be a "person of the book" as you work on a Christian worldview.

4. *When you choose a college to attend, think about it in terms of developing your ability to think and see.* In other words, if you're thinking about a Christian school, find one that integrates faith and learning, where Christian professors are dogged pursuers of truth and love the Lord as well. Or if you're thinking of a state college, look for a fellowship group where faith and studies are discussed and integrated, where you can be supported when you struggle with some of these issues.

5. *Go overseas for a while.* It's tough to develop a *world* view without traveling. Almost every college or university has some sort of travel program, and often a quarter or semester overseas will not cost significantly

Thinking "Christianly"

more than staying on campus. If you can't afford a semester, you might take a summer to work overseas or to serve on a mission team. If your church fellowship doesn't have a mission team, check with other campus fellowship groups or see some of the resources given in chapter sixteen.

When you travel, go where you'll be stretched. Don't go with eighty of your friends to Avignon, for example. Try out the University of Jos in Nigeria for a semester instead.

6. *If you can't travel right now, get involved in some local, cross-cultural ministry or establish friendships with international students.* If your campus is near a city of even moderate size, there are ethnic pockets and people that you can get to know by working or volunteering. Check out tutoring programs, volunteer as an aide at the local Boys and Girls Club, or teach English as a second language. Even at home you can get to know other cultures and ways of life.

7. *Keep up on national and world news.* Skim through a good newspaper and read one news magazine faithfully. Since my junior high years, I have been reading *Time* magazine. Of course, all magazines have a bias, and *Time* is no exception, but regular reading has kept me aware of the world's needs. Reading a magazine in the midst of heavy academic demands takes commitment, but it's one way to break out of the monasticism of college life and broaden your world.

8. *Read some Christian books.* To add even more reading when you have a heavy reading load throughout the quarter may seem insane. But budget some time to read outstanding modern Christian authors like C. S. Lewis, Simone Weil, Francis Schaeffer, Flannery

O'Connor, Robert E. Webber, and Chuck Colson. Think about the classics as well: John Bunyan, Augustine, Calvin, Luther, and many others.

9. *Stay spiritually fit.* (See chapter three.) You can be current, alert, and updated. You can travel, visit, and serve. Being a well-rounded person may give you a worldview, but not necessarily a Christian one. By staying spiritually fit, by reading the Word, by walking with the Lord, a *Christian* worldview will emerge.

10. *Find a mentor.* Begin a relationship with someone who is older, wiser, and stronger in his or her faith. Go to that person for advice, support, and accountability.

11. *Keep working on it.* There will be painful times for you when you're working on your beliefs, when what you've heard in a class seems to seriously threaten what you have held tightly in the past. But be willing to ask tough questions and to ride with some of them unanswered for a while. Persevere.

12. *Share what you know.* Dialogue with people, speaking what you believe and know. The give and take of speaking and listening will help you clarify and sharpen your beliefs. If questioned and you don't know the answer, say, "I don't know." Then try to work out an answer for yourself.

13. *Think globally, eternally, strategically.* Realize that you can make a long-term difference in the world. (That's part of your Christian worldview!) Throughout history, students have been on the frontlines of almost every great spiritual movement. Just over one hundred years ago, the Student Volunteer Movement broke out in the Ivy League. Over the following thirty years, nearly 20,000 of the finest young American and British college graduates took what was known as "The Princeton Pledge": "It is my purpose, if God permits, to become a foreign missionary."

A Cornell grad who became the first chairman of the Student Volunteer Movement wrote these words: "Let us be satisfied with nothing less than leaving the deepest mark on our generation."

One person who made a lasting mark was a young woman from Northern Ireland named Amy Carmichael. She sailed to southern India. Over the following five decades, she and her organization rescued hundreds of children from the painful humiliation of Hindu temple prostitution. Here is the prayer she prayed for herself. May it be our prayer as well as we think like a Christian and see the world like God does.

"From prayer that asks that I may be sheltered
from winds that beat on Thee,
From fearing when I should aspire,
From faltering when I should climb higher.
From silken self, O Captain, free Thy soldier who
would follow Thee.
From the subtle love of softening things.
From easy choices and weakening.
Not thus are spirits fortified. Not this way with
the crucified.
From all that dims Thy Calvary, Lamb of God,
deliver me.
Give me the love that leads the way.
Give me the faith that nothing can dismay.
Give me the hope that no disappointment tire.
Give me the passion that will burn like fire.

Let me not sink to be a clod.
Make me Thy fuel, Flame of God."

14. *Relax.* When we read a prayer like Amy Carmichael's, our reaction might be either to quit school and head for southern India or consider her one of God's *big* heroes and put her in a category that we think we could never achieve. Categorizing people like her also distances us from uncomfortable challenges and comparisons. But we should neither quit school nor consider her life "heroic and unattainable." God has us at school. He wants us to refine our thinking and make a difference in the world. But he is also a wise, loving Father who doesn't burden us with loads too heavy to carry. He gives us times to relax, to play, to enjoy exploring the world he made. So be diligent in thinking but enjoy your college career; make a difference but still play, praising the Lord as he prepares you and shapes your worldview.

Thinking "Christianly"

CHAPTER

5

TIME MANAGEMENT
In a Multiple Choice Life

One of the hallmarks of maturity is the ability to manage time well, to determine what is really important, to schedule time to get the important done, and then to do it. This process of time management sounds so simple, yet it's very complex when one lives in a multiple-choice life.

No one is born with an innate ability to manage time well. Some people seem more naturally organized than others, but time management is an acquired skill that takes diligence and perseverance to master. Like any skill, time management requires learning the fundamentals, and then these fundamentals must be practiced and applied. Learning to ski, play the piano, or paint all require fundamentals, practice, and application. But where these other skills aren't always necessary in college, time management is crucial to college survival.

In college, you must manage your time even more strictly than ever before. You may have had demands in high school, but the demands were usually not as involved or intense as in college. Options abounded in high school but not to the extent that they do in a university setting. And in high school, a person's parents usually helped in the structuring of days and in the control of time. But in college a student is on her own, so time management becomes a crucial skill.

If you were a good time manager in high school, you have an advantage. But you're moving to a new level of increasing demands and your present skills will need to be honed. If you were a poor time manager in high school or if someone else usually managed your time, you have a challenge ahead of you. You're going to have to grasp the basic skills fairly quickly and apply them immediately.

Early in your college career is the perfect time to take the opportunity to schedule effectively, because the sooner you get started the better. The fewer bad habits like sloppiness, procrastination, tardiness, and laziness you develop, the fewer bad habits you'll have to break. My friend Mark Preslar says, "Your life is made of time. When you waste time, you are wasting your life. Lots of people have great ideas, but only if you learn to be disciplined with your time can you make your ideas a reality."

Begin *now* to be a time manager. Effective time management skills will help you gain the most from your studies, give you more time for what you deem important in college, and prepare you for the world beyond college. Corporate employers and admission directors at graduate schools are looking for those who effectively manage their time.

We'll touch on several time management tips as we look at how to study in general and how to study for specific subjects in particular. But for now, here are nine general time management principles for college survival.

1. *Plan ahead.* "An hour spent in planning saves three or four in execution." That's an old time-management adage that is absolutely true. Planning is not wasting time; it's saving time. Whether you're looking ahead a day, a month, or a year, whether you're preparing to take a test, write a paper, or prepare a meal, plan ahead.

2. *Give God a portion of your day.* As you plan

ahead, make God your top priority. In chapter three on spiritual survival we discussed ways to make God a priority, and one way to give God priority is to schedule a daily quiet time with him. Then include time in your schedule for Christian worship and fellowship throughout the week. Putting God first may seem like a backwards way to plan when you have so many other demands and especially when a quiet time may not seem as urgent as other options. But there is a distinction between what is urgent and what is important, and time spent with God is important. Rod Handley, a successful student and now an exceptional minister to students, said to me recently, "I've seen time and again what can happen when I choose to honor the Lord with time during my day and what happens when I leave him out. By giving Him time, God multiplies my day. All of a sudden I'm blessed with an extra hour or two I didn't expect. Plus I find I'm much more productive. When God is left out, problems occur for me; I'm sluggish, anxious, worried, impatient, and easily frustrated. So giving time to the Lord is the greatest thing I can do to manage my schedule." If, like Rod, you give the Lord a portion of your day, God will bless the remainder of your day with his presence.

3. *Determine your other priorities.* If you've followed suggestion number two, you've basically said that your

relationship with God is your number-one priority, because you've given God first shot at your day. But what else is important to you? Academics must be high on your priority list because that's one of the major reasons you're in school.

But if push comes to shove, which courses are most important? In other words, where do you need to spend most of your study time? Courses in your major are usually more important than ones that aren't, and because of the grading system five-unit courses are usually more important than two-unit courses. Obviously not all classes are created equal.

Besides having academics as a priority, your health also needs to be a priority. You need to decide when to sleep and how much sleep you need. And you should also schedule exercise time.

Social life is another important priority. After being alone with the books, it's both relaxing and stimulating to share ideas and spend time with friends, so be sure you schedule some social activities.

Think through your priorities—academics, health needs, and social life—and then give time to those things that are most important to you.

4. *Get a calendar.* To help you schedule your

time, buy a small calendar or daily planner to carry with you to class. There are many models on the market, but I recommend those with a place for daily planning and an address and phone section.

5. *Use a calendar to plan a daily and weekly schedule.* There's a difference between buying something and using it. After you've purchased a calendar, put it to use. Think through the average day: When do you want to have your quiet time? When do you need to go to class? When do you want to exercise? Enter those times in your schedule. And remember to give yourself a quiet hour (or half hour) when you can be alone to collect your thoughts and focus your energies.

After scheduling daily activities, look at your weekly commitments. Schedule time for your dorm activity, your intramural game, and your club get-together. Next, look ahead at the month. What papers are due when? When are your tests? When are the big social functions you don't want to miss? Mark your important commitments in red ink so you can spot them quickly. Finally, look at the quarter or the semester. When do you want to go home or take a mini-vacation? When do you have spring vacation or a reading recess? When's Mom's birthday? Mark those dates.

6. *Use a daily priority list.* In addition to scheduling your day, write down the top priorities for the day. Some people call this list a "to do" list.

I suggest that you create your priority list the night before. In the evening before you go to bed, take ten or fifteen minutes to write down your most important tasks for the next day. After you've listed them, put them in order of priority, either by putting a number beside each one on the list or by making a new list with the tasks listed in order of priority.

Then, during the day, work on the most important task until it is done. When you've succeeded, cross it off your list. (The act of checking it off gives you a sense of fulfillment, completion, and mission accomplished.) Then start on the next one. Don't skip items or do only the easiest tasks; instead, do the most important tasks, giving your time to the top priority items.

7. *Don't overschedule.* You can do too much, scheduling yourself until you feel like there is not a minute to relax. Resist the compulsion to overschedule.

There will always be more than you can ever do, more options than you can select. So practice saying no to opportunities and demands. A good way to say no tactfully is, "I would really like to do this, but I must say no; I'm overcommitted already." Such an answer is honest and shows you're a person with priorities.

By not scheduling every minute of your day, you'll be open to times of spontaneous fun with friends, and you'll be able to fit in unforeseen circumstances and interruptions.

8. *Know your prime time.* Prime time is the time when you function best. You may be a morning person. If so, try to take your most difficult classes and study your most important assignments in the morning. If you're an evening person, schedule your evenings so you can tackle your top priority items then. In either case, you will accomplish more if you study at your prime time. Work *smart* – not just hard and long.

9. *Don't say yes to every request.* An old Russian proverb says "Friends are the thieves of time." Your buddies will always have a good idea to help you avoid studying. Sometimes you should take them up on the idea and get away. But don't look at every opportunity as something you must do. You can't do everything, so learn to say no.

As you go through college, you'll add other principles of time management to your list. But for now, concentrate on these suggestions as you manage your time and your life.

SECTION

2

LIFE IN THE
CLASSROOM

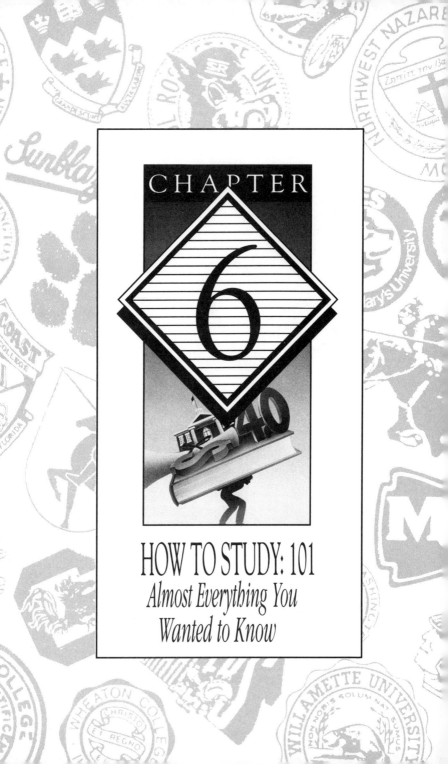

CHAPTER

6

HOW TO STUDY: 101
*Almost Everything You
Wanted to Know*

I t's crunch time in this book. In the next five chapters you'll be plunging into academics – the world of classes, home-work, problem sets, reading, writing, testing, lab reports, and study groups.

For some people, academics energize. These people go to college to learn, to expand their minds, to test their intellectual abilities. They glory in the mere pursuit of knowledge.

For others, academics open doors. They enter college already anticipating future prospects of a job or career. Such people view college as a stepping stone to success and prosperity in the "real world."

For still others, academics serve as a side dish at the banquet of life. College is football, socials, relation-ships. This kind of person does a minimum of studying in order to participate in a maximum of extra-curricular activities.

Regardless of your approach to college and to academics, study skills enable you to survive and to succeed. If you are at the university to pursue knowl-edge for knowledge's sake, you will learn more if you know how to study. If you are at college to get a job in the future, study skills will help you raise your grade point average and impress your future employers. If you are at school simply to enjoy the social life, study skills will enable you to *stay* there. The results of good study skills are that simple.

So let's start with some general study principles and move to specifics. And remember as we proceed that studying is learning how to *acquire* necessary knowledge, *organize* it, and *apply* it in a practical way to a specific circumstance. Here are some points to help you acquire, organize, and apply your newly-acquired knowledge.

1. *Know yourself.* You need to know yourself in several areas to be a better student. First you need to know *what subjects you are inclined toward.* The subjects that come easily to you are usually those you can do well in and those that require less time and effort than other classes. Writing, literature, and psychology classes fit this description for me. Other classes will give you more difficulty and will require more of your time. Foreign languages and science courses fit into that category for me. Sometimes you will do well in many different courses, and then you will need to decide which courses you enjoy most and pursue those.

Next you should find out *where and how you normally study best.* Time and place can dramatically affect your studying abilities. I mentioned already in the last chapter how "prime time" is that time when you function most effectively and the time when you should be doing your most important tasks, including studying for those crucial courses. But you should also be sensitive to where you can best spend that prime time. Do you study best in a quiet room or a noisy coffee shop? Do you function better when others are studying around you, or do you find the library distracting and prefer to study in solitude? You need to find the studying environment you're most comfortable with, because there will be times when you absolutely must get something done and choosing the wrong location or time will make it more difficult than it already is.

For example, I was a morning person, not a night owl, in college. I did not do well in all-nighters. So I tried to take morning classes and did my studying in the early afternoon and evening. I preferred studying in my room when my roommate was gone, because I didn't like the library much. I found that when I was comfortable with my studying place and studying time, I accomplished much more.

Finally, as part of knowing yourself, *determine your goals and then concentrate on the courses that will help you best realize your goals.* For instance, if your goal is to become a C.P.A., it's more important to do well in your accounting classes than it is to do well in art history.

2. *Be aggressive.* Like it or not, you are part of the TV generation. You have learned since you were a child to sit passively and absorb information. But absorption is not the learning style you'll need to succeed in college. You will need to be much more aggressive in your learning.

Aggressiveness begins in choosing classes. Shop around. Find out as much as possible about the course and the professor. Go to the department and ask questions. Meet the professor if you can; introduce yourself and ask questions. Talk to students who have taken that class. Bear in mind that a good instructor can be much more important than the time when a class is offered. A good instructor can inspire you and greatly increase your chances of success.

Continue that aggressive stance after you're in class. Talk to the instructor after class. Make appointments to see the professor or teacher's assistant if you need to. Ask questions; then listen aggressively.

Whether you are listening to the professor, studying by yourself, working with a study group, or reading class material, think and debate aggressively. Follow the train of thought and reproduce it in your own words. Look for accuracy in logic and for clear language. And look for the true and the false in what you read and hear.

Be aggressive in reading and in note-taking. Whether you are writing in a notebook or reading a book, write your own thoughts on the page. Save a third of the page vertically in note-taking so that you can write your own thoughts beside the notes you've taken, or so you can make notes *on* the notes when you're studying for a test. If you listen, study, and read aggressively, you will soon make every book you read or lecture you hear a part of yourself.

Here I should add a caution about underlining: Don't highlight or underline everything. Instead, underline key words and facts, and do some writing in the margin. If something is surprising, jot a huge exclamation mark in the margin. If a point is directly relevant to a test or a paper you are working on, put a star beside it. If something is unclear, draw a question mark. If something seems stupid or illogical, write "stupid!" A mere word or two will help you capture your thoughts on the point.

You can be aggressive not only in your study habits, but also in controlling your interests. If your program requires you to take a class that doesn't interest you, get aggressive with the class, thinking of ways in which this knowledge and skill may be helpful to you in dealing with people, in pursuing your career, or in better understanding the world around you.

Acquire a vision of how this class fits into what you're doing now or what you'll accomplish in the future. Talk to your professors about the subject and find out what makes them interested in the subject. Your chance of success improves when you're most interested in something, so work at it.

Finally, you need to aggressively control your emotions. Realize that you are not the servant of your emotions. You may feel bored with school and depressed about studying, but this temporary feeling will escalate if you procrastinate instead of facing your feelings and pushing through them. If you persevere, studying in spite of your emotional ups and downs, your discipline will be rewarded.

However, if you find that whatever is making you depressed is more serious, be aggressive in seeking help from a fellow student or pastor or counselor.

3. *Be enthusiastic and positive.* In addition to being aggressive, be enthusiastic. You need to read and listen analytically and critically, but do so with enthusiasm. If you are an attentive, active listener, giving the professors good eye contact, they will note and appreciate your attention, especially in a class where students are looking bored.

In note taking, don't write *everything* down—just the highlights. Otherwise, you won't be able to listen actively. If the lectures contain truckloads of specific data, try bringing a tape recorder, then listening to the tape later for the details. But beware: Don't turn on the recorder in class and then fall asleep. You *still* need to listen. And don't forget to listen to the tape ASAP after class; if you get behind in reviewing the tapes, you'll never catch up.

4. *Know what the class requires.* Some classes are graded very objectively, and class participation doesn't count for much. But other classes where the grading is more subjective will require more of your active participation in class. So look not only at tangibles like papers and tests as ways to make the grade; look also at the intangibles: your attitude, your actions, your participation. Discover *exactly* what you'll need for a 4.0; then find out how much you can miss and get a 3.0. Treat each individual class as a game that has a new set of rules and objectives; find those rules and play by them.

5. *Know your work load and stay on top of your classes.* Avoid last-minute cramming if at all possible. Spending some time daily on each course will eliminate the need for an all-night catch-up session before a midterm or final. Besides, cram time usually isn't as productive in memory retention as learning the material gradually and reviewing it over a longer period of time. Those who have paid their *daily* dues are the ones most prepared for tests.

Calculate the number of pages per week you'll have to read for each course by simply taking the number of pages in the book assigned and dividing them by the number of weeks. Or follow stringently the page numbers your professor lays out for you to read, and if you spot a crunch later in the week or month, read ahead for that class. Each week, check to see whether you're on top of your reading in all your classes.

Make large, longer-term assignments a priority even though the weekly quiz may seem like a big deal. Learn to estimate how long it will take you to do a three-page, five-page, or ten-page paper and budget time weekly for that. Write down deadlines for everything in your calendar and review those deadlines at least once a week. If you follow all these hints, you will stay on top of, not under, the pile of schoolwork and papers.

6. *Establish a routine.* Have a time that is devoted each day to studying only. Let there be no question in your mind or anyone else's that this is *study time.* Have a routine place to study. If you have a routine established, you will spend less time and effort each day in making decisions about study place and time.

7. *Attend classes; don't skip them.* Attending class gives you an edge. The professor just might say something helpful on a day when you aren't there. You've paid a lot of bucks to be there, so show up.

8. *Get to know your professors and teaching assistants (T.A.'s).* Knowing your professor will help you when you need answers to some puzzling questions in class. Also, professors can be invaluable in the future in recommending other good courses in the department, in writing a reference for you in a job application, or in offering advice about your major. And if your professor or T.A. has trouble speaking English, it's advantageous to meet with him during office hours in order to clarify whatever you didn't understand.

9. *Do all your homework as it's assigned.* Students run into trouble when they procrastinate on homework or don't take it seriously. Homework has been assigned to help you internalize the principles of knowledge and learn by doing. Football coaches like to say, "You play like you practice. If you work hard from Monday through Friday, Saturday will take care of itself." The same principle applies to doing homework. If you neglect homework, it will come back to haunt you on test day. The work may seem monotonous, but it must be done.

10. *Look for opportunities to score "extra points."* Often professors will give extra points for special projects done outside the classroom, homework being turned in on time, or class attendance. Find out about extra points and work to score them. All the extras add to the grade and can make a difference in moving from a 2.9 to a 3.0 or more.

11. *Study in chunks, not bits, of time.* Don't try to study in fifteen-minute blocks only. Give yourself some long chunks of time, especially when studying difficult subjects. But also utilize shorter periods of time. I know students who carry their bookbags with them everywhere in case they get some "surprise time" when they can study.

12. *Take study breaks.* Study for fifty-five minutes and then take a five-minute break for a little physical activity (running, stretching, or throwing clothes in the washer). This break will help you maximize the rest of the time you study. Or go for two hours and take fifteen minutes to get a cup of coffee. But break up your study time. Breaks will refresh and renew you and serve as a reward for being a diligent student. They also give you a reason for not procrastinating. Three hours of study seem overwhelming. But almost anyone can work hard for fifty-five minutes.

13. *Live as balanced a life as possible.* Relationships, physical exercise, outside class interests, sleep— all help you live in balance. People who are balanced are usually able to handle the demands of study better than those who live one-dimensional existences.

14. *Form a study group.* Form a study group if a course is especially difficult and important. Choose other students who are successful, who will push and challenge you. When you prepare an assignment or study for a test for that class, divide essential topics among your study group members, having them work in their specialty areas. Then give brief presentations at the next study session. The very fact that other people are counting on you is a great motivator, and this principle of dividing and conquering will help you understand the material and give you the discipline necessary for good studying.

15. *Get a tutor if you're totally stumped.* If the study group isn't working for you, and if your professor and T.A.'s don't have the time to help you, get a tutor. Check with the department and ask for recommendations, or look for your college's study skills center, a place that will set you up with a tutor free of charge.

16. *Begin each study session with prayer and praise.* If you begin your study session with the right attitude, an attitude of praise rather than depression, you will accomplish more and even enjoy what you are doing. God wants to be foremost in your mind so that he can give you the peace and confidence necessary to good studying. So trust God in this area of your life and commit your study time to him.

17. *Reward yourself when you've finished a project, test, or course.* Most people don't need to be told to celebrate an accomplishment, unless they are so worried about the grade that they forget to feel relief that the work is over. Remember, the fact that you finished is accomplishment enough, so reward yourself.

Now, in the midst of all these suggestions, I will add number eighteen, a comment from Doug Early that just might destroy everything I've written earlier. But I will include his suggestion nevertheless.

18. *Find what works for you and do it.* Doug says, "I personally never wrote a rough draft for anything I ever wrote in college, and I did well. Perhaps I could have done better if I had spent more time preparing, but I don't think so. I *thrived* under pressure. Sometimes I procrastinated, but that was what I needed. Several times I tried reading short segments over a period of days, highlighting as I went. Another time, I tried writing short bits of a paper. It didn't work for me. I had no concept of flow, of wholeness. For me, writing a paper and reading for a class consisted of 'going for it.' I worked best going for huge blocks of time and never stressing the minor points. Not only did I never prewrite, but I also never underlined while reading. One argument for not underlining is that it draws attention away from other details, and often in reading you need a sense of the whole."

I personally don't think everyone can follow Doug's plan and survive, but he did. He had a way that worked for him.

19. *Give academics your best, but also relax.* Take the points written above, weave them into your life, find what works for you, and be an aggressive, good student, a person with sharp study skills. But remember that God doesn't love you based on what grade you received for the day. Thank God that he never bases his love on our accomplishments but on our relationship with him through Jesus Christ.

In the next four chapters, we're going to continue this academic theme. First we will look at the tasks of writing papers and taking tests, and then we'll jump into three specific areas of study: the humanities, the sciences, and the arts.

CHAPTER

7

TAKING TESTS &
WRITING PAPERS
Constant Companions

Maybe I was weird, but I liked taking tests in college, especially if I was prepared. Tests were a challenge, and I was the competitive type. I liked going head-to-head with others in class and seeing where I stood. I got a charge out of seeing what I could recall and explain.

I enjoyed the recognition that came from my professors and my peers when I scored well. I liked games, and test taking was a game to me. The preparation. The slight nervousness as the professor handed out the exam. Then the game itself with the score published later. And finally the sense of relief and accomplishment when the test ended. To people who dread tests more than anything in the world, I probably seemed strange.

On the other hand, when I wrote papers, I understood their feeling of dread. Writing papers was not a game to me as taking tests was, but I wrote them nevertheless. And I found that some of the secrets to both successful test taking and paper writing were the same: planning ahead and being organized. But there are some other principles of success as well, that I will cover in the following points, so let's move ahead.

Test Taking

How to Prepare

Most of us can't expect to perform well on a test unless we've prepared well in advance of the day of the test. The key is in organization and good study habits. Organize the course so that you can recall it better. Start with the professor's way of organizing the course and see how everything fits into a general outline derived from the syllabus or the notes you took in class. Or organize everything around the scheme of the text. Presumably the professor and the authors know enough about the subject to fit the facts into an orderly, logical framework. Every fact that you have to know for a test should fit somewhere within that scheme, and knowing the organization will help you to study and recall those facts.

Part of this preparation involves creating a study strategy. One strategy that Andrea Swart, a 1988 graduate, used in school for a Friday test went like this:

a. Have all the material read by Tuesday at the latest.

b. On Wednesday, read over and study class notes and problem sets. Talk to the professor or T.A. if you have any questions.

c. On Thursday afternoon, meet with study group.

d. On Thursday evening, go over readings and anything else that you need for recall.

Your plan might be different from Andrea's, but you get the idea—plan ahead.

Keeping in mind the organized, plan-ahead motif, let's look next at how to study for specific types of tests.

Taking the Closed-Book Essay Test

Here is Mark Hogendobler's game plan, a strategy that will help you put your notes and facts into logical order:

1. *Read your course notes thoroughly only once,*

and make an outline of the course. Put in every pertinent fact whether you understand that fact perfectly or not. If you aren't sure whether to include a fact, keep in mind that you won't be going back to your notes again. As you do this initial recopying, leave room to add information from the texts where appropriate. (By the way, this exercise in writing is called kinesthetic learning. You are learning through your muscles and your eyes as you write. Kinesthetic learning may be more beneficial to you than simply reading or reciting to yourself or to others.)

2. *After you've gone through your lecture notes, add the notes that you jotted down in your text.* (**Note:** If the professor relies mainly on the text, take notes from the text first and from the class lectures second in this initial outline. But if the professor presents most of the information through lecture, follow this method and go to your lecture notes first.)

Do not go back to your text or notes again except for occasional reference. Now you have a compact, easily understood set of notes to study.

3. *The next step in the "gospel of study according to Mark" is to go through this first set of revised notes and make a new, shorter set of notes, eliminating facts that you have learned.* Keep doing this revision and summary as often as you need to, not trying to memorize everything at one time. After writing several sets of notes, you should have only statistics, numbers, formulas, and dates that you simply have to memorize rather than understand. Memorize that last set of notes, and you'll have the course in the bag.

Now let me add a few other points to Mark's game plan.

4. *When you get to class, make sure you have the necessary materials for test taking:* pens or pencils, blue books, calculator, and anything else your professor may have required.

5. *As soon as you receive the test, read it over quickly.* Determine how much time you have for the test and which questions are worth the greatest number of points. Then begin, writing first on those questions worth the most points. But give yourself time to write on each question, for sometimes even a short paragraph can score more points on a question than you expected. No answer at all gives the grader no choice but to give you no points.

6. *As you approach each question, develop an outline of key points you want to cover.* I sometimes did that in the margin. Then proceed, writing legibly enough for the grader to be able to read your answer. My cursive writing was so poor that I printed my answers; you may need to do the same.

7. *If you have time, read over your answers to correct grammatical and spelling errors, to add a point, or to check your facts.*

Mark adds this last bit of advice to those facing closed-book essay tests: "Restrained and well-chosen verbosity can do wonders. Be assertive about what you are saying even if you're not so sure that it's absolutely correct. Put as much information down as possible and do your best to make it all seem like a necessary component of your argument. Draw on sources outside the course. Professors love that. A key word in writing essays is *justification*. Always justify your answer. In science courses, your answer might be different from the professor's answer, but if it is well documented and justified, the professor may give you partial credit because of your justification. A good professor will always want to see all of your work anyway, and that is why essay tests are often easier to do well on than multiple choice. If you simply show how much you know, you should be able to conquer the essay test."

8. *Turn in the test.* Walk out of the room and give yourself a standing ovation.

Taking the Open-Book, Take-Home Test

Mark also offers some suggestions for taking this type of test.

1. *Organization, once again, is the key.* You may need to review your notes and organize them in your mind, but in this case you can usually stop with the second set of notes described above. Where you proceed from here will depend on the course and the type of test. An English literature take-home test may have you digging back into your texts. But an exam in science may require you to have the formulas and facts well-organized and at your disposal, or you may need examples from previous tests and lectures to use as models for your new answers. Physics and organic chemistry often require knowing a generalized statement or formula to solve problems of a specific type. And biochemistry may have you preparing enormous flow charts of all the reactions in a particular pathway. In science courses, some essay tests ask you to design experiments. Make sure that you have all the proper tools at your disposal. Learn the techniques in advance—and well. And remember: Most scientists have heroes. If you can drop some names of these heroes in the exam, it helps (e.g., "...as Gregor Mendel demonstrated in his backyard experiments on sweet peas"). Graders will, more often than not, be impressed with general knowledge in your field of study.

2. *Before you begin, read over all the questions carefully.* If you misread the question, you'll strike out on the answer.

3. *For each question, ask yourself: What is my main point going to be and how will I approach it?* Your refined study notes (described above) will help you on the organization. Developing a simple outline will also help you here.

4. *Write your essay as you would a paper,* including an introduction that explains what you'll be writing, a body of solid facts and thoughtful opinions, and a conclusion that wraps up your essay in a satisfying manner.

5. *When you've finished writing, reread the whole essay a couple of times, making corrections as needed.* If the professor allows, have other people read the essay and give honest suggestions for revisions. My coworker, Sue Harris, who graduated in 1988, suggests that you type the final draft since take-home tests are expected to be better written and "cleaner" than in-class essays.

Taking the Multiple-Choice Test

1. *If you've gone over your notes and the text and developed a set of study notes, you'll probably have all the information you need for a multiple-choice test.*

2. *When you're first handed the test, skim it quickly so you know what's coming.* Budget your time. And then begin.

3. *Generally, you should stick to your first choice as your answer.* Unless you've misread the question, your first answer will usually be the right one.

4. *Answer all the questions, even if your answer is a total guess.* And if you are completely in the dark, select option "c." Researchers tell me that's the most popular correct answer. But the best way to get the correct answer is to eliminate those answers you know to be false and then guess. You have a better chance of guessing right when there are only two options than you do when there are five.

5. *Sue adds, "If you're using one of those "fill in the bubble' forms along with the test, fill in each bubble answer as you come to it.* Never wait until you've answered each question to go back and fill in the bubble. You may run out of time."

Taking Oral Tests

1. *Prepare for oral tests as you do for in-class essays, reviewing and condensing your notes.*

2. *Practice answering questions out loud.* Start by answering questions alone, then have a friend listen so that you get used to speaking to another person.

3. *Look presentable, sitting tall and doing your*

best. And be confident. You'll often know more about your subject than your professor does, especially when you defend a thesis or long-term project.

Suggestions for Taking All Kinds of Tests

Jim Allen, a 1987 graduate who excelled in the field of psychology, suggested these points that will help you in taking any kind of test, whether oral or written.

1. *Be aware of clues in the questions.* Sometimes you can find the answer to one question in the wording of another question. Be observant.

2. *Don't be afraid to ask clarifying questions during the test if you're confused about the question.* However, make sure it's the T.A. you're asking and not one of your fellow students!

3. *"State Dependent Theory" says that you should take the test in the same condition in which you studied for it.* In other words, if you were tired and wired on coffee, take the test tired and wired. Jim said he did it this way and it worked for him. But I always liked to be well-rested when I took a test.

4. *State Dependent Theory also claims that the best place to study for a test is the*

room in which you will take the test, because certain parts of the room may trigger an answer in your memory.

5. *People who tap their feet during a test do significantly better on exams than people who do not.* Why? Probably because more blood circulates to their brain than to the brains of those who sit still. Jim likes the results of this research because he's a toe tapper.

6. *Don't cheat.* The amount of cheating that goes on may seem overwhelming to you. It may seem like you'll never be able to get grades as good as those who cheat, but for Christians it's important not to cheat. Jim says, "I struggled with cheating until I realized that anything God wanted to do in my life wouldn't require my cheating to achieve it. If it's God's will for you to be a doctor, you don't need to cheat on your chemistry exams to make sure you get into medical school. If you trust God and his love for you, you won't need to cheat."

Finally, in all tests, I also encourage you to pause before you begin and commit the test and your recall to the Lord in prayer. He loves you and is concerned about everything you do—including test taking.

Writing Papers

In writing papers as in taking tests, organization and planning are the keys. But here are specifics for those papers you'll be required to write. I've asked Kim Ebeling, a 1988 graduate in psychology and a Phi Beta Kappa, to add her thoughts to mine in this section.

1. *Choose your topic.* Pick a topic that interests you since you will be spending considerable time on the paper and since you tend to do better work when you are involved and interested. To get ideas for a topic, look over your notes, browse through the library, or consult with your professor. You'll probably want to check with your professor to make sure the topic is acceptable and not already assigned to someone else.

2. *Gather your sources.* When consulting with your professor about your topic, also ask him or her about resources you could include in the paper. Then go to the library and familiarize yourself with its system and its personnel. Some libraries store their information in card catalogs; others use computers to help you find books. In either case, don't be afraid to ask the librarian for help in finding a resource. And don't limit your resources to books alone; interviews, magazine articles, newspaper articles, and government publications can often be just as useful in your paper as books. These publications are often listed on special microfilm machines or in published indexes such as *The Reader's Guide to Periodical Literature.*

3. *Take notes.* Use 3 x 5 or 4 x 6 cards to take notes on your sources, writing down only one basic point of information on each card. Your notes may be summaries, quotations, paraphrases, or personal comments on the material. In any case, be sure to document your source so that you can include its reference in your paper.

4. *Write a thesis statement.* As soon as possible, while you are still doing research, write a thesis statement—a one-sentence statement that summarizes the points you want to make in your paper. For instance, suppose you're writing a paper about American colonists. Your thesis statement might be: "A strong faith in God and his direction in their lives both motivated the colonists to settle in New England and sustained them through the early, difficult years."

5. *Write an outline.* The major points of your outline should relate directly to your thesis statement, and your research will develop the outline. For example, working from the thesis statement given above, your outline might look like this:

I. Desire for religious freedom in Europe
  A.
  B.
II. Faith in God Maintained through the Hardships of Travel
  A.
  B.
III. Four Major Adversities in the Early Years and the Colonists' Response
  A.
  B.
  C.
  D.
IV. Conclusion

As you build the outline, use key words or phrases that will jar your memory to bring back thoughts when you begin to write. Under each key point write an example or other documentation that supports, clarifies, or exemplifies what you are trying to say. Write on your research cards where each point will fit into the outline.

Writing an outline may seem like unnecessary work, but in fact a carefully worked outline will give your paper clarity and organization, helping you to stick to the point and to move smoothly and logically from one point to the next. So don't neglect the writing of at least a rough outline.

6. *Write a rough draft.* Using the outline as your guide, write a rough draft of your paper, not worrying at this point about grammar or punctuation. Instead, just get your thoughts on paper. Don't be concerned if halfway through you decide that point #8 should be point #3. You can worry about that later. Double-space for later editing.

7. *Take a break.* Do something that will free your mind from the paper. If you have the time, "sleep on it" and come back to it the next day. If you don't have the time, take a least an hour break and shoot some hoops, listen to music, or do anything that will clear your mind. Gaining some distance from the paper will enable you to see it with a clear, critical, editor's eye.

8. *Edit your paper.* For your first edit, read the paper whole to get a feeling of its overall structure. Put question marks where the paper doesn't make sense. At this point, this is what Kim does: "I go back through the paper and on a separate piece of paper, I write the number of each paragraph and one sentence that describes the gist of the paragraph. This gives me time to look at the big picture. If a paragraph seems out of place, I move it to another place where it makes more sense, or I delete it. I also add transition sentences where necessary." Following Kim's comments will help you to do your first edit, which is for *organization.*

Your second edit is for *grammar, punctuation, and word choice.* Concentrate on each sentence, asking yourself these questions: Is the sentence complete?

(Sentence fragments should only be used for stylistic reasons, not out of carelessness.) Is the sentence punctuated correctly? Does the sentence fit into the paragraph? Could you say the same thing in fewer words (Generally, the less wordiness the better; good writing is usually clear and concise.)

9. *Have someone else read your paper.* Take your paper to the college's writing center, discuss it with your tutor, or show it to a friend. Outsiders will often catch the flaws you failed to find simply because they have distance from the paper. They can help you greatly by putting question marks in the margin if the paragraph seems unclear, by writing comments on the paper, and by catching your grammatical flaws. You should, of course, choose your critics carefully, finding readers who are fairly skilled in writing and who will be honest with you.

10. *Type the final copy.* After you type the final copy, you may want a friend to proofread it for you to catch any typos. Since professors are no different than other human beings, often judging on appearance as well as on content, make your final copy as clean as possible. The less your professor is distracted by surface flaws, the more he or she will be able to appreciate the

content of your paper.

To make the whole process of writing, revising, and typing a paper easier, use a computer. Most colleges have set up computer centers where students may type their papers. Check into this service early in the semester and master a basic word processing program. The time you spend learning how to compute will pay off later as you write and revise your papers.

11. *Appreciate what you've written.* Not only has the paper helped you in your grade, but the research has given you greater insight into the subject and you've improved your writing and research skills as well. Whatever the grade you receive, you will also learn from the professor's comments, so don't toss the paper when you get it back. Carefully check each marking and comment to make sure you understand what they mean and how you can improve in those areas in future papers. Then appreciate how writing this paper has made the next paper just that much easier to write.

Tests can be fun and papers can be rewarding— *if* you don't wait till the last possible moment to work on them! But if you plan ahead, organizing your thinking and writing as you go, you may even learn to enjoy these twin tasks.

What kind of tests you take and what kind of papers you write will vary depending on your field of study. So next we will discuss three fields of study that require some specialization in survival: the humanities, the sciences, and the arts.

CHAPTER

8

LIFE IN THE
HUMANITIES
Subjectivity at its Best

Doug Early, a friend whom I've mentioned before, graduated from the University of Washington in 1986 with his B.A. in English. He spent his first year out of college teaching English in China and is now in graduate school. A veteran of the humanities, he offers this characterization of this field of study: "If a person's only r eason for going to college is to get a well-paying job in the future, I don't think he or she is going to fit in well in the humanities. You have to go into the humanities because you want to *learn*. You want to learn more about yourself, human beings, the world around you."

Humanities focus on the world around you because, by definition, humanities are the branches of learning that focus on culture. College and university catalogs vary in their definition of the humanities, but we usually understand humanities to include history, literature, writing, philosophy, and religion.

I was a psychology major in college. At my alma mater in that era, psychology seemed to reside more in the humanities than it did in the sciences. In addition to my psychology classes, I took many of my elective courses in the humanities, courses like English literature and creative writing. For the most part, I loved those courses for involving me in stimulating discussions, for giving me a better understanding of life, and for providing me with the opportunity to read many great writers. I'd advise anyone who is in the sciences, business, arts, or education to take electives in the humanities. You won't regret the time you spend there; the courses will enrich the rest of your life.

But enter the humanities knowing that you enter the land of subjectivity. Perhaps no other school is so subjective as the school of humanities; every aspect is affected by subjectivity: the courses, the content, the professors, and the grading.

This subjectivity can work against you unless you use it to your advantage. So be subjective yourself and take classes that *interest* you. Of course there are classes known as "G.P.A. builders," but don't look for those classes as much as for classes that really interest you. Doug Early says, "I firmly believe from *personal* experience that you will usually do better in a Survey of Milton class than in Speech and Hearing Sciences 200 (a G.P.A. Builder) if you're *interested* in Milton."

One way to increase your interest in a class is simply to take an interesting professor. Often you will have to take required courses that don't automatically pique your interest, and in that case, getting a certain professor is especially important. So find out the reputation of professors by talking to older students and department advisors. Then talk to the professors themselves to find out what books you'll be reading and how the course will be taught.

When you finally choose a course, you should combine all this outside advice and information with what you know about yourself. What is your learning style: Are you a discussion-oriented or lecture-oriented person? My wife, for example, is a person who learns more from discussion than she does from straight reading or pure lecture. What are your writing strengths: Do you prefer to write creative or analytical papers? The most important thing to know about yourself, however, is how much you're interested in the subject. If you're strongly interested in a particular subject, give it a shot unless your advisors—people who have been there before and who know you— shout a resounding, "Don't do it!"

I emphasize interest again because it can take you a long way in enjoying and actually learning from the course. Interest is necessary for doing well in any course, but the humanities require an extra amount of interest. In order to read so many novels, write so many papers, be ready for so many intense discussions and still eat, sleep, exercise, and function like a human being, you have to love what you're doing. You have to love plunging into Shakespeare or Kant or Augustine. Doug says, "I love reading Shakespeare. I love discussing existentialist philosophy, or the impact of Marx, Darwin, and Freud on nineteenth-century literature. If I didn't love it, I'd die."

Doug's point is: If you're going to be involved in the humanities, you'd better do it because you're interested. Otherwise, the amount of work and the subjectivity of it all will overwhelm you.

But if you do decide to study in the humanities, you will benefit from the following "humanities study tips" on reading, discussions, writing papers, and taking tests.

1. *Read everything carefully and thoroughly.* Since the bulk of your work in the humanities will usually consist of reading, make sure you don't get behind. Getting behind will force you to speed read, skim, or not read at all, and playing catch-up doesn't allow you to linger over the text, to think about what you've read. And because your discussion, papers, and tests will be based on your reading, you won't do well in class unless you do your reading.

As you read, be the aggressive student I talked about earlier. Ask the author questions. Argue with the author. Write your comments and questions in the margins, and sparingly underline key points and passages. The more you involve yourself in the text, the more the text will give you.

When you are reading poetry, you need to involve yourself in a slightly different way than when you are reading a history text or a novel. Poems pack a multitude of meaning in a minimum of words, and in order to mine all the meaning you can, you need to read the poem several times. First read through the poem one time without stopping in order to get a sense of the whole. Then read through it again slowly for allusions, metaphors, alliteration, and all the other literary techniques and details. On the third time through, read the poem aloud to see how the words play against each other like notes in music. Finally, read it silently one last time, thinking of all the facets you have just uncovered in your previous readings. Most poetry will explode in meaning for you when you

put that much work into your reading.

Like poetry, other types of literature hold most of their meaning below the surface, often in the play of words, and usually in the interplay of character and situation. Sometimes, to the inexperienced reader, nothing seems to be happening on the surface, and that reader will think the work boring. But you should never underestimate a writer or a work. Generally, professors have chosen writers who are important, who use an interesting style, or who have something relevant to say. Read carefully. If it seems like something is missing or out of place, note it and ask yourself, why? What was the author trying to do there? Don't rush yourself when reading literature. Give the novel, play, or short story time to linger in your mind and senses. A good work of writing leaves a wonderful, lingering aftertaste, and during that aftertaste you will usually make the most substantial discoveries.

2. *Get involved in class discussions.* Discussions provide excellent personal growth opportunities as well as a chance to learn more from the course. Not only do you learn from the comments of other students and the professor, but you also learn how to express and argue your own opinions. And if you have a good professor, don't be afraid to disagree with him or her. Doug told me that he once had a different interpretation than one of his professors on a traditional Scottish ballad because of some lyrics that Art Garfunkel added when he made the ballad into a contemporary song. Doug said, "I explained my interpretation—and this is the key—by supporting it with direct quotes from the work. My professor was a giant in the college. She had been teaching for over twenty-five years and had been teaching this ballad throughout her career. She was so taken aback that she said she needed to go home and think about it. The next class she told me she thought I was correct. It opened a whole new reading of the ballad for her. And it did wonders for my confidence as a student."

Come prepared for discussions, having read the material thoroughly and having thought through what questions might be asked. Be as well-prepared for the discussion times as you would be for a paper or a test.

3. *Have a vision for your paper.* Before you touch your pen to paper, or your fingers to the word-processing keyboard, before you even begin, know how you're going to end. Have a vision of your paper as a whole before even starting on the parts. That vision will sometimes drive you forward, and you'll write till you finish. Or that vision will sustain you so that you are able to write, stop, and pick it up again later because you know where the paper is going. But without that vision, your paper will shatter into shards of disjointed facts and opinions.

As you write, never say for yourself what the author can say for you. Your job as a writer of papers is to use evidence from the work you've read to come up with a conclusion. Whenever you state an opinion, support it with specific excerpts from the work. If you can't find any supporting evidence, your opinion is probably invalid. But make sure you *have* an opinion. (Humanities are subjective, remember.) And whenever you use excerpts, explain why you're citing that passage and how it fits into your overall argument.

If you're uncertain about a paper, talk to the professor or other students you trust. Most professors would rather help you *before* they grade your paper than after.

4. *Show what you know on your tests.* Tests in the humanities assess whether you've read the material, thought about the material, have opinions on the material, and can substantiate your opinions with the material. Most professors are not impressed by the length of your answers. They are more impressed by clarity in thinking and in writing. Having legible handwriting helps also; if your cursive penmanship looks like a medical doctor's, print your in-class tests and type your take-home tests. But the most important thing in test-taking is to show that you have struggled through the material and made it a part of you.

One final word: If you are a mad scientist (the subject of the next chapter) or a business major (chapter ten), still take some courses in the humanities. This is the chance of a lifetime to sit with men and women who have lived their lives in the humanities and who are excited about their field of study. Learn from them. Interact with them. You'll be a much better, more well-rounded person for the effort. And you'll look back with thanksgiving at an opportunity not missed.

CHAPTER

9

THE MAD SCIENTIST:
Life in the Labs

When I left high school, I was determined to be a psychiatrist. Why? I don't really know. I had never met a psychiatrist and had only seen a few in movies. But I was interested in psychology, and I thought the psychiatrists' medical training helped them do more for a patient than a psychologist. Plus I liked the idea of being a medical doctor.

So I decided to major in psychology and prepare for medical school at the same time. I had taken the usual physics, chemistry, and biology courses in high school and had done well. I had also done fairly well in math—up to a point. As a high school junior, trigonometry and calculus had given me problems. Even so, my grades had been good, and upon my arrival in college I was tossed into the honors chemistry program.

I got blown away in that class. For several reasons, I just couldn't cut it. One, I was a freshman not used to studying hard in a field where I wasn't having much fun. I always did better in subjects I liked, and I didn't like chemistry much. Two, my attitude toward the sciences wasn't as good as it was for the humanities. Three, my desire to be a psychiatrist didn't match the effort needed to get there. Four, I was playing too much Ping-Pong. My day would go like this: up, classes, some study, basketball practice, dinner, and then a tough, best four-out-of-seven Ping-Pong match with an intense competitor from Oregon. My Ping-Pong skills improved immeasurably during that quarter, but my chemistry grades didn't. I got a C and was light years behind my fellow classmates who were highly motivated types. And I decided that maybe I would just be a psychologist and forget the psychiatric thing.

I tell you about my scientific history so you'll know I'm not the Mad Scientist. I did take anatomy and physiology later and got A's, but I'm not the expert we need for this chapter. So I recruited some experts to help me out: Jim Francese, a 1986 graduate from Cornell University in chemical engineering, and Mark Hogendobler, who graduated from Princeton University in 1987 in microbiology.

Jim says, "Studying in the sciences is fun but challenging. It's a unique way to go through college. While some of my friends were planning menus in the School of Hotel Management or reading about the Vietnam War, we were taking pictures of colliding hockey pucks in the physics lab or spending sunny afternoons trying to separate and identify chemicals the teaching assistants had maliciously mixed together perhaps only hours before. Strangely enough, I really enjoyed it. I liked learning more about how God's universe works and the intricate, orderly way he has put it together. The friendships formed during those years were enhanced by the long hours we spent together working on labs and problem sets. In purely practical terms, I was able to get a good, useful education. Even if I do not stay in the field of chemical engineering, I believe that my scientific background will benefit me in any job in any location."

Science courses are different from the humanities, the arts, and the business courses you might take. The labs, the technical literature, the terminology, and the background learning required make life in the sciences complex. In addition, the sciences are intensely competitive from the beginning. Even in introductory chemistry or biology courses, there is often a competitive air because many potential medical school applicants start worrying about their grades (and justifiably so) their freshman year. Science majors also face more required courses, so they don't have as many electives to take as other students. And often the workload is very heavy. In other words, the mad scientists need all the help they can get. So let's begin to look at the characteristics of the sciences and explore how to be a better student in this critical area.

The Technical Lecture

Science lectures can be boring. What could be worse than someone droning on endlessly in polysyllables about cell walls or the John Doe equation or cow stomachs? This tediousness is compounded by the fact that many scientists who teach are not as gifted in communication skills as their colleagues in literature and speech (although you can get gifted communicators and poor communicators in any major). But, as in every course, consistent attendance at lectures is important. No matter how unskilled or boring the lecturer is, the exposure to the material is invaluable. Copying notes from someone else is not the same as hearing the words yourself and seeing your professor write the facts on the chalkboard or overhead.

Professors also use their lectures to give you clues regarding the approach they will take on the next test, or they'll give hints that will help on your current homework assignment. The fifty-minute investment in

the class lecture can save hours in doing the homework assignment or pay off with a ten-point increase
in your grade on the test because you heard the clues.
Jim says, "Often professors will assign huge amounts of
reading but only lecture on portions of it. It has been
my experience that what is emphasized in the lecture
is emphasized on the homework assignments and
exams. Thoroughly learn the parts of the text the
professor talked about, and give a more cursory treat-
ment to the pages he omitted."

Another reason for attending class is that professors are quite good at knowing who is sitting in the
lecture hall and who is not, even in fairly large classes.
Very few professors actually take attendance, but they
are uncanny at making mental notes of who's there
and who's not. If your attendance is poor, they will be
less likely to boost your grade if you're on the C+/B-
border, and they probably won't give a sympathetic ear
to your explanation of why
your lab report is late. In other
words, showing up for the
lecture helps your relationship with the professor.

It's also useful to
prepare for the lecture
ahead of time. Most pro-
fessors want you to read
the assigned material
before they lecture on the
subject. Be prepared—
and stay conscious. The
benefits of attendance
diminish significantly if

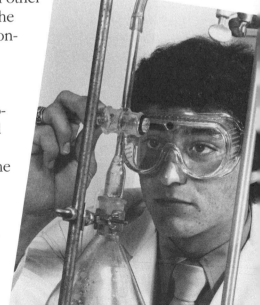

you are neither prepared nor awake.

In class, make an effort to adapt to the lecturer's pace for note-taking. Some professors write very quickly on the board while talking continuously. A sensitive lecturer may slow down if you ask, but lecturers often feel they have too much material to cover and must race constantly through the quarter or semester, so note-taking can be difficult. A shorthand system is helpful. Abbreviate frequently used words with the first letter of the word or some other symbol. Some students bring their textbooks to class. If the instructor is drawing a mammoth diagram on the board that is also in the book, you can write "see page 154" in your notes and save some time and writer's cramp. Some other tactics: use colored pens to help you interpret graphs or find equations at a later date. Jim knew someone who bought a stamp of a benzene ring and would stamp his notes instead of drawing it each time the professor drew one on the board. (Look up benzene ring in your dictionary: "A structural arrangement of atoms...marked by six carbon atoms linked in a planar symmetrical hexagon..." I can see why you'd want to make a stamp of it!)

If you can, ask questions in class. Many students are reluctant to ask questions for fear they'll look stupid, but if you are confused about something, others probably are too. Don't let pride keep you from raising your hand and asking a question. Jim, who is naturally reluctant to ask questions, says he prays for courage and humility to overcome this intimidation because he knows asking the question will help others as well as himself. When in doubt, ask questions. When afraid, pray.

The secrets to gaining from science lectures are simple: Attend, stay awake, listen to clues, take notes, ask questions—and buy a benzene ring stamp.

Technical Reading

Pound for pound, scientific textbooks are more expensive than choice steaks, fine seafood, and sports cars. One *paperback* book required for your upper-level anatomy class can cost you $50. That's expensive. But there are several ways to combat the high cost of textbooks.

1. *Buy used books.* Most campus stores have supplies of used books that are sold for considerably less than new ones. But to get the best used books, you need to get to the bookstore as soon as you arrive on campus for the semester or quarter. (As my pastor's mother used to say, "We need to get in line first before the greedy people do.") Sometimes the students themselves hold a used book sale at the beginning of the term. Again, these sales are known for their long lines, so arrive early to get the pick of the pack.

2. *Borrow the book from a friend who has previously taken the course.* This strategy will end up being a disadvantage if you want to mark up the book, but it does have the advantage of saving you money. Since your friend invested a lot in the book, you may want to repay your friend for its use, and if your friend is fussy about a book's condition, you'll want to take good care of the book.

3. *Share the book and split the cost with another student.* This is tricky because you both may want to use the book at the same time—especially when test time rolls around. Sharing a book may be more complicated than it's worth.

4. *Find out how much the book will be used.* If there are several expensive books listed as required reading, check with the professor on how much he or she will be using each textbook. If one text turns out to be relatively unimportant, you might be able to use a library copy of that text.

Once you have purchased or borrowed the necessary texts, here's what you do next: *Read the books!* Many people don't read the books, or they simply read enough to do the assignments. What they don't realize is that material not directly relevant to the specific task at hand can help in a broader understanding of the subject matter. And that broader understanding can aid you in tests later and even in a future job. Most students grumble at one time or another, "I'll never use this stuff." They're probably right. Most stuff won't be used. But as a student you don't know what stuff will be used and what won't, so you'd better read.

What's the best way to read technical works? The answer is the same that you've read in these pages before: Do whatever works best for you. Highlight with a fluorescent marker and make notations in the margins. Or underline and take notes as you read. Some people write in pencil, especially if they plan to sell their books. The important point is to read in a way that enables you to learn most effectively and prompts the most accurate recall.

Keep in mind that it's one thing to *know* the subject matter, but it's another to *communicate* it. Some scientists don't have great literary skills, so don't be surprised if you find that some of your textbooks are hard to read or poorly organized. To overcome this difficult problem, try referring to another textbook on the same subject to see how another author tackled the material.

When the course ends, you're faced with the difficult question: Do I sell the book or keep it? The temptation to sell may be great, especially when your cash supply is low and the people down the hall have just had a pizza delivered. But textbooks from even 100 or 200 level courses can be valuable resources later in school. A senior in your major can tell you which books have proved especially useful. Another general rule: If you are considering graduate school or medical school, it is a good idea to keep those books that relate directly to your field.

Homework

1. *Find a friend.* In the sciences there is much to be gained from working with a friend or a study group. Often science assignments are long and difficult, requiring many calculations and applications. You may be able to do 90% of the work on your own, but the other 10% may escape you. A classmate can help you with the parts causing you difficulty, and you can do the same for him or her. And even if you have a good understanding of the material, working with someone else can give you added insight and a new perspective. Plus, when you get bored or exhausted, you have someone to go out with for coffee or ice cream.

Working with someone on assignments doesn't mean you have to discuss every point of every problem. There will probably be long moments of silence as you work together. Working together might be meeting a classmate at the library to do the assignment so you can help one another out if needed. Such arrangements also hold you accountable. The time lost to procrastination will decrease if you know you have to meet someone and get the work done at a certain time and place.

2. *Find a Christian friend.* If possible, choose a Christian classmate with whom to

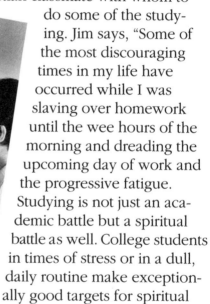

do some of the studying. Jim says, "Some of the most discouraging times in my life have occurred while I was slaving over homework until the wee hours of the morning and dreading the upcoming day of work and the progressive fatigue. Studying is not just an academic battle but a spiritual battle as well. College students in times of stress or in a dull, daily routine make exceptionally good targets for spiritual attack. Typical responses in such times are selfishness, irritability, and seeking to blow off steam through fleshly means. The enduring truth of Jesus Christ is powerful enough for any situation. His grace is sufficient to keep us walking with the Spirit on a continuous basis. Spending study time with a brother or sister in Christ will be a constant reminder of the eternal perspective we have."

3. *Use the T.A.'s.* T.A.'s are an invaluable resource. In many classes, the only time you see the professor is during the lectures and exams, and the rest of the work is done by the T.A.'s. They will be the ones grading most of your papers and teaching the homework and review sessions. They are being paid to be helpful to the professor and to you, so use them. If you are having problems with an assignment, do not hesitate to see them during their office hours. Again, don't be afraid of seeming stupid. You can save a great deal of time by asking questions instead of stubbornly trying to solve a problem that you don't have the background to solve.

To approach a T.A., you need to understand T.A. psychology. Most of them are graduate students who have been assigned to the course and may not be that excited about it. They may also be feeling the pressure from their own workload. For example, Jim and Lisa Francese got married in the late summer following his first year in graduate school. He returned from their honeymoon four days before fall classes started and found that, in his absence, he had been assigned a notoriously time-consuming T.A. post for the upcoming quarter. In addition, he was taking one difficult class and had three research projects in progress. That's what many T.A.'s are facing, and the result is that they don't let themselves appear approachable or friendly. But they *are* there to help. So schedule an appointment during their office hours. If they can't answer your question, ask them to recommend a source you can pursue to find the answer.

Studying for Tests

In the sciences, you study by working on problems, writing up lab reports, and reading material for the first time. At some time, however, you will need to review and memorize the material for a test. Jim says, "Studying for tests was perhaps the most distasteful study task for me and was the most likely to get pushed to the bottom of the priority list. But in retrospect I can see it was quite silly to spend time working on a homework assignment worth about 2% of my grade when I should have been studying for an exam worth 15 or 20%."

To study for a test in the sciences, follow these suggestions:

1. *Review lecture notes.* In studying for an exam (and again, studying with someone can be helpful), review your lecture notes. If you listened carefully, you probably have indicated what the professor noted as particularly important in the lecture. Concentrate on this material.

2. *Compare your lecture notes with what is in your textbooks.* Any material covered in the lecture but not covered in the text is probably an item for a test. If the professor has lectured on material not in your textbooks, he or she felt that these concepts were important enough to use as a supplement and they will probably appear in the exam.

3. *Review graded homework assignments and your lab work.* Before you walk into the testing room, you should know how to do all of the assigned problems without looking at the solutions even once. You shouldn't just memorize the solution itself, but should master the concepts involved in reaching the solution.

It is difficult but necessary to move beyond the *specifics* of sample problems done in class and assigned in homework to the *general principles* involved. Scientific textbooks can be full of problems, diagrams, equations, and charts. Ask yourself what physical processes or phenomena are being described. Are there any equations, charts, or diagrams that look similar to the one at hand? If so, what is the common link? If you cannot describe in words what ideas are being expressed by an equation or what the purpose of an assigned problem is, then you do not have a thorough understanding of the general principles involved. Jim says, "I can think of a blatant example from my own experience. I failed a math exam because I had merely familiarized myself with how to do all the homework problems instead of really learning the material. When I got to the test and had to be creative in solving new problems instead of regurgitating old ones, I fell flat on my face."

4. *Do extra problems.* Most textbooks have numerous problems and questions designed for student use, but only a few are assigned. Attempting these extra problems will give you a greater familiarity with the material. If you're really motivated, you can even go to different textbooks on the same subject and try a few problems there.

5. *Some courses require brute memorization.* Gradual learning is the best way to memorize a lot of material. If you have a test coming that requires a lot of memorization, start reviewing a week in advance, a few pages at a time, fifteen minutes to a half hour every night before you start your other work. In this manner, you will have several hours of study time already completed before you start the final push the night or two before the exam. Trying to memorize a lot all at once is a painful ordeal, and you will most likely forget most of the facts soon after—or, worse yet—during the test!

6. *Take some study breaks.* Your mind will appreciate the recess, and you'll be more efficient when you sit back down to study. At Cornell, there was a mass exodus from the undergraduate library around 9 p.m. nightly, because that was when fresh cookies came out of the oven at the Student Union. Isn't it amazing how food and study go together in college—and how most students put on weight! When I was in college, we'd take a break and have Oreos and a quart bottle of Squirt. I haven't had that combination since. Instant sugar high.

Other breaks: a quick game of power nerf basketball, Olympic paperwad throwing championships, a quick walk around the block. Study breaks such as these help reduce stress and ease the tension that builds during a long study session, especially when a deadline is approaching. I personally recommend a 55/5 approach: fifty-five minutes of studying and a five minute break.

7. *With all courses, don't leave Jesus Christ out of your studying.* Jim says, "Over the years, the most important ingredient to a successful study session has proved to be the submission of my work to the Lordship of Jesus Christ. He desires to be in charge of everything: every lab, every homework problem, every reading assignment. Apart from Christ, our lives and our work have little significance. I have experienced supernatural abilities to learn and write and be creative when I have prayerfully given the tasks at hand to the Lord. More importantly, He is pleased when we do this. He has given me great joy in what could be considered dire circumstances. Give your work daily to God and you will be amazed at the way He works in things the world considers mundane and ordinary."

Good advice.

Life in the Lab

As a mad scientist, you'll spend many hours in the lab. You'll begin to think of it as home. So learn to make the most of that lab time—and, once again, the key is preparation.

1. *Read first.* Science instructors often make reading assignments that are to be completed *before* you begin your lab session. There's a reason. That reading probably contains important information about theory, equipment, and procedures that your instructor thinks you ought to know in advance. It may even include warnings about dangerous parts of the procedure. But many students don't read those preparatory assignments, often because they're still working on their lab reports from the previous week. Says our man Jim, "I walked into many labs barely knowing the title of the experiment we were doing. If the T.A. had told me we were making meatloaf that day I probably would have volunteered to chop the onions."

Don't fall into that habit. It's frustrating to have to ask the student next to you or the T.A. about every step of an experiment. Lab periods can get very long that way. And if the person you ask is wrong, your experiment will be ruined. So make it a habit, before every lab session, to at least skim the suggested reading. If time allows, make an outline of the experiment's goals, procedures, hazards, and expected results.

2. *Take great notes.* The laboratory notebook is your record of experimental preparation, the experiment itself, and your subsequent analysis and conclusions. Most students record their preparation and analysis just fine. But they don't do as well in recording the actual experiment. It's disheartening to be struggling to finish a lab report the night before it's due, only to find out that you're missing key data or observations.

Why does this happen? Because students put too much faith in their own memory. It's difficult, a week later, to recall what shade of blue your solution was or what the fish liver looked like. Jim says, "I prefer to write down everything in nauseating detail. It will take longer to do the experiment if you are very thorough in your notations, but trying to recreate experiments from memory is a near impossibility."

3. *Write with as much clarity and neatness as possible.* Writing up lab reports, like many other college tasks, is easier done in groups. Sometimes the questions you're expected to answer based on your findings seem to require a Ph.D. Several people working together are more likely to arrive at intelligent responses than one person relying on his or her own limited knowledge and insight.

If you performed the experiment with a lab partner, you may be expected to write the report together. In that case, be a responsible lab partner. It's discouraging to be part of a "team," and end up doing 75 percent of the work.

Mark Hogendobler says this about writing lab reports: "Get examples of lab reports written by former students who have done well in the course. Follow them scrupulously. You can't be too neat or too precise in a lab report. Define everything. Use lots of footnotes. Don't be afraid to include stuff that you think is important but that might not exactly belong in the report, either because of space limitations or because of the professor's specifications; just put it in appendices at the end. Figures take a long time but if done correctly can add megapoints to your score. Use a Macintosh or other computer to draw them. A neat report, even though it may be imperfect from the standpoint of content, will usually receive a better grade than a technically perfect but sloppy one."

Mark was a 4.0 student. Listen to him.

4. *Proofread.* Eliminate spelling and grammatical errors. That, of course, is easier said than done. It's hard to spot errors in your own writing. It helps to put the report down and work on another task for a while before proofreading. Or maybe you and a friend could proof each other's. Beware of the "wee still hours of the morning effect." It's amazing what makes sense to you at three a.m. Proofread in broad daylight, when you're wide awake.

5. *Enjoy your classmates.* Lab classes provide a great opportunity to spend time with people and get to know them. Pray for the people with whom you work in lab. These opportunities can lead to great friendships and a chance to share your faith.

That's life in the sciences. Now let's move out of the laboratory and into the studio as we look at the arts.

CHAPTER 10

STUDY POTPOURRI:
The Arts, Foreign Languages,
& Business

In the four preceding chapters, we focused on one of the major tasks in college survival: studying. We first looked at general study principles, then explored the specific skills required in the humanities and the sciences. But there are still other subjects with their own study and survival skills, skills that must be mastered in order to succeed. These subjects include the arts—music, drama, dance, painting, sculpture, and more—foreign languages, and business and accounting courses, which sometimes seem to employ a foreign language all their own.

Let's look at some of these particular areas of study.

The Arts

Let's begin with the arts. We'll talk particularly about music, drama, and the visual arts. My sources in this field are Scott Burnett in music (an '82 grad), Laurie Wheeler in drama (an '89 grad), and Nancy Seifert in the visual arts (an '87 grad).

My sources tell me that the arts are even more subjective in their professors and in their grading than the humanities. In the arts, performance is judged primarily on the personal taste of the professor, and if you don't know his tastes well, or if you're not appreciated by that professor, you might be in trouble.

In addition, you might take some grief from your peers or your parents for majoring in an area that seems so impractical. "How will you get a job as an art major?" is a question you may hear more than once. And those questioners are partially right. A degree in music or art is not necessarily the ticket to monetary gain or cultural fulfillment. Scott says, "Don't be a music major if you can do anything else. It's not easy—and if it is easy, you're in the wrong school. It's even harder when you get out. There is no job for a music major unless you are in music education. And if you do get a job, you may not be able to use your musical skills in the way that you wanted."

Nancy adds, "I think of all the persecution I took for not having a 'real major.' In my heart I knew I was doing the right thing *for me*, but I felt guilty when midterms or finals came along and I didn't have any. But those late nights forcing my creativity into a project due the next day were just as bad as or worse than studying for a final. I poured my soul into my art and each piece became a testimony of my faith and my struggles."

Both Scott and Nancy know from experience that involvement in the arts requires an enormous amount of commitment. You must pour yourself into the arts because almost every other person majoring in your field is. The artist's life is intense, and you need to be dedicated to survive.

In the midst of this intensity, you'll sometimes wonder whether what you're doing is worth it—or even whether God approves in light of everything else that's happening in the world. These types of questions happen in other fields of study, but with the arts the questioning may be even more acute.

Scott Burnett, who attended a Christian college where there was a strong emphasis on missions, felt the pressure to abandon his music. He says, "I struggled with the question, "Why am I sitting by myself in the practice room six hours a day, when thousands of people in the world are dying of starvation and thousands of others need to hear the gospel?' I had to deal with the subject of my 'personal calling'; had God given me gifts in this area, and did he want me to pursue them? If he did, I needed to sit in that practice room for six hours a day. God called some people to feed the hungry and share the gospel, but right now, God had called me to sit and practice."

Nancy Seifert, who attended a secular school, felt another form of pressure from her friends, who wondered how she could be part of the "artsy" crowd. Nancy answers, "One day it became clear to me that I did have a purpose in being part of the artsy crowd. That day in class we shared our larger-than-life outdoor sculptures. Most of the people in the class had created very bleak and angry projects, but my sculpture celebrated my faith and my Creator. Art helped me express the joys, questions, and struggles of my heart. And it was worth it when my professor told me, 'I do not subscribe to your beliefs, but I respect the way you express them.' Being an art major was not easy, but I felt like an ambassador for Christ there in that part of the university."

The field of drama holds even more intense pressures than the music or visual arts fields, for it is difficult to maintain a strong Christian walk in the midst of the theater world. Laurie Wheeler warns, "Entering the arts without a complete understanding of how theater in particular will attack your faith parallels a toddler walking into a lion's den to pet the big kitty cat. It's naive and stupid, and you will be slaughtered."

What are particular ways in which theater will attack you? One is the attack of self. Christians are called to put God above self, but in theater you are constantly pushing self as you fight for auditions and push your way to prominence. If you can't get the roles, you can't get the credit.

Then there is the attack of what Laurie calls "the two great naivetes." They are: (1) Theater is a harmless institution that provides entertainment to people and (2) When an actor plays a part, it's only a character—there's no reflection of the actor at all.

First, Laurie argues, theater is no harmless institution, nor, like literature, is it an entertainment-only medium. Playwrights present their views of life on stage just as novelists present their views of life in books. Whether the medium is written or visual, it presents messages, many of which are antithetical to Christian beliefs.

Second, playing a role is complex. Acting realistically requires that an actor or actress become the character. Playing hate requires *feeling* hate; playing lust requires *feeling* lust. Laurie says, "I've played characters that give in to lust and hatred, and the ease with which those emotions emerged through the character frightened me. More frightening was the difficulty of submitting the sins of hate and lust to Christ's control in my daily life when I was submitting to the sins in my theatrical life. Your character becomes real; it seems to become a part of you. So where does the Christian draw the line?"

To deal with these pressures, Laurie gives her profession to the Lord. She trusts God to help her to say no to roles she feels are wrong for her, and she trusts God to provide roles she can play. Before, during, and after every rehearsal Laurie prays, and she also memorizes Scripture to counteract the lines she learns in the play. Laurie seeks Christian friends outside the theater crowd to hold her accountable, to keep her from getting caught up in the unreal world of theater. And finally, Laurie strives to glorify God by playing her role to the best of her ability.

If you feel called to drama, or to music, or to the visual arts, trust that God will give you the strength to resist the pressures in the arts, and then give him the glory in whatever you do. The pressures may be intense, but know that the power of God is strong within you.

Foreign Languages

There is a Russian proverb: "When you learn another language, you gain another soul." Acquiring a language gives you a powerful tool for interacting with people, but it also gives you another way of viewing the world and another way of expanding yourself.

No matter what your major interests are, a foreign language can literally and figuratively open doors for you. There are many opportunities for students to go abroad and study in almost every country of the world, and there is even

financial aid available for such travels. Mark Preslar, a student who is working on his Ph.D. in the Russian language, says, "Students with sufficient language skills often can receive financial aid to study almost any subject in a foreign country. The first two times I went to the Soviet Union, my trip was partially underwritten. My third trip was completely paid for and on the fourth one, still academic, they paid me!"

With Mark's help, let's look specifically at study and survival skills in the field of foreign languages.

1. *Distinguish between language learning and language acquisition.* There is a difference between language *learning* and language *acquisition,* even though both processes are at work when we are gaining language skills.

Learning involves a conscious effort to master the grammar, vocabulary, and rules for using the vocabulary. Some researchers feel that this type of learning contributes little to one's ability to speak a language, but this knowledge does help us to understand the language and monitor our speech.

The acquisition process is different. The language skills we *acquire* come to us in speaking and understanding. To activate the built-in device that helps us acquire language, we simply need to supply our brain with large amounts of meaningful, interesting language input at a level slightly above us. If we spend one hour memorizing a verb conjugation, we will have memorized a verb conjugation, period. But if we listen for one hour to a speaker who is speaking only the target language (the language we want to learn) and who uses the verb conjugation repeatedly while she discusses something important to us, we will acquire the skill to use that verb conjugation in real language situations. In summary, to acquire the language, we need to saturate our minds with the language.

2. *Make an attitude adjustment.* Researchers have defined an "affective filter" that can limit the amount of language a person can acquire. The filter consists, to a large extent, of the student's attitude and emotions. The affective filter (the things that affect and hinder our ability to acquire language) goes up when we are anxious, worried, and self-conscious. The less we worry about what other students think or about what mistakes we will make, the better we'll do. "Plan on making language mistakes," Mark stresses.

Because I had a high affective filter, I never did well in foreign languages. In my high school French class were two upperclassmen I really admired: a great basketball player and a gorgeous cheerleader. I didn't want to make any mistakes in front of them, so my language skills suffered. In college, I didn't give Russian my best shot. At that time, I wasn't so much worried about how I was doing as uninterested in what I was doing. To really acquire a language, you have to be interested and involved in that language.

If you are interested in what you are hearing and learning, you will be focusing on the content of the message and not on the form of the language. Consequently greater acquisition will take place. Mark advises, "When you are listening to the language you want to learn, always concentrate and strain to understand. If the language seems above you sometimes or you realize you are not picking up much, never turn off and start daydreaming. If you do that, you will get nothing. There will always be things you do not catch or understand. Do not let that worry you. Choose to be interested and to concentrate, and always have your notebook ready to write down interesting expressions. Whenever possible, write down your thoughts in the language you are learning, even when the thoughts seem simple."

3. *Expose yourself to the language.* In order to learn a language, you must expose yourself to it. Take advantage of your college's language labs; listen to records and tapes of people speaking in your target language. Make tapes of your professor speaking in class. Then tape yourself speaking the language. The important thing is to inundate yourself in the language as much as possible so that soon you will be thinking and even dreaming in a foreign language.

Exposing yourself to the written language means reading your material through several times. A Russian proverb says, "Repetition is the mother of learning." If you listen to a tape several times, you will find that it becomes easier to understand. The same goes for reading; if you read a story through several

times, you will soon piece things together. Mark says, "After you read a text through once, look up some words in the dictionary, but don't stop there. Go back and read the text again as many times as is practical and interesting. You will then reinforce your knowledge of the new words and acquire more of the language."

There are also enjoyable ways of increasing your exposure to a language. Watch a movie in your target language or, better yet, study the language in its natural setting. If your college doesn't have an overseas program in that language, other colleges do, and often you can easily transfer the credits. Because of the exchange rate, you will sometimes pay the same or even less to study abroad as you would pay to live and study on campus. So research the study-abroad opportunities available and take advantage of them.

4. *Find out about the professor in advance.* If at all possible, before signing up for the class, find out about the professor's teaching style. Be sure the instructor uses the target language in the classroom either exclusively or almost exclusively.

5. *Go to class and be an active participant.* Listen extremely closely when the instructor is speaking in the target language. Most language instructors speak the language at the correct level for a student to learn, a level slightly above your current level. As you strive to understand as much as you can, do not mentally translate the words into English. Instead, just try to get a feel for what is going on.

6. *Get help from a tutor.* Find a tutor or a native speaker as a resource, but do not use them to help you with grammar. Instead, talk to them with your tape recorder running, and have them talk to you. Interview them, asking them questions in areas that interest you and letting them talk about areas that interest them. At first a conversation with your tutor may be frustrating, since they do not know how much you can understand. But if you can keep working with the same person, he or she will get to know your language abilities and will instinctively tune their speech to your level.

7. *Learn individual words by learning phrases or key expressions.* There are times when you *must* memorize words and their meanings, verbs and their conjugations, nouns and their declensions. This is part of language *learning,* and it is important! But the best way is to learn words in phrases. Then you are not only getting the word by itself but also a ready-to-use chunk of the language that is couched in its proper environment.

8. *Finally, be passionate about language.* You have seen that language acquisition requires time, energy, and repetition. To acquire the skill you want, you'll have to be passionate and dedicated to your language and spend plenty of time with it daily. It is best to get your assignments done as early as possible, but completing assignments is not enough. Mark says, "You must devote extra time to the language if you want to excel, no matter how brilliant you think you are. Just before bed and when you first wake up are good times to read lighter stories in your target language or to listen to tapes. While jogging or commuting you can listen to tapes or review flashcards. Combine whatever other interests you have with the language you want to learn. Beginners can usually find 'readers,' books with built-in glossaries and dictionaries and sometimes with simplified texts. These are good because they get you started. But when you read texts without glossaries, don't look up every word in the dictionary. Instead, concentrate on reading and see how much you can recall. If you spend time reading and enjoying the language, you will train your memory, and language acquisition skills will increase immeasurably."

We've spent enough time on languages. Now let's move to our last speciality field.

Business, Economics, and Accounting

Rod Handley, our primary source for this section, graduated with a degree in accounting and spent four years working as a C.P.A. with Ernst and Whinney, one of the big eight accounting firms.

Rod says, "One of the things I appreciate about this field of study is that what you learn in the classroom applies to real life situations. The examples used in a classroom may be slightly idealistic, but for the most part, they are true of life in the business community. My approach was to learn basic principles such as supply/demand theory, organizational management, debit/credit entries, and so forth. Then when I went to work, I was amazed at how much these theories actually did apply to business."

Now here are some guidelines for this practical, application-oriented field.

1. *Do the homework.* These classes are notorious for piling on repetitive, often boring assignments. But it's important to keep up for several reasons. First, the homework will help you understand a concept or theory. Second, usually this homework constitutes a certain percentage of your total grade and to avoid the work or "borrow" the answers from a buddy will only hurt you in the long run. Third, the homework builds upon prior knowledge. Missing yesterday's work will compound the difficulty of today's assignment. Getting behind adds to the confusion. So be sure to set aside time daily to complete the work.

2. *Don't wait until the last minute to cram.* In some college courses you can cram. Here it just doesn't work. As stated in number one, these courses build on one another. To try to cram in an all-nighter is a great recipe for failure.

3. *Look for internship possibilities or other ways to put your knowledge to the test in a practical, hands-on way.* Some of the most productive learning can be done on a summer or part-time job. Even working as a cashier at a fast-food franchise can be beneficial. If you keep your eyes and ears open to the business side of selling Big Macs, you can learn a lot. Rod says, "Experience is important because I found that my professors and textbooks assumed that I knew generally accepted business terms such as a *general ledger.* Theoretically, I knew what a general ledger was, but only when I did an internship with an accounting firm did I learn how a general ledger worked and why it was such an important document. Any kind of business experience will impress a future employer and give you an edge in class."

4. *Be aware of trends and schedule some classes accordingly.* For Rod, the trend was in computer knowledge. He didn't realize in college what an impact computers were having in the business community. When he got out of school, he was behind in the area of computers and had to play catch up.

For example, a recent trend you might want to consider is the tremendous influence the Pacific Rim nations—Japan, South Korea, and Taiwan—have on American business. To prepare yourself for dealing in that marketplace, you may want to take some classes in Asian studies or international trade.

5. *Finally, get a well-rounded education.* First, get a well-rounded education in accounting and business. Rod says, "Many of the people I met while serving as an accountant lacked understanding of basic business terms. While in college, I suggest that you concentrate on getting a well-rounded assortment of classes. Then, as you study, constantly ask the question, 'Why?' Why is this statement important? Why does this theory work this way? Your future employer won't expect you to know every single item about their particular product, service, and methods when they interview you, but they will expect you to understand basic theories and principles that will support their efforts to be profitable. Your employer will spend time and money training you to do exactly what they want you to do on the job."

Second, get a well-rounded education beyond business. Rod notes, "The successful business people I met were people who had a well-rounded background. They weren't necessarily the bookworms, but they had many diverse interests."

Some of these pointers for business majors probably sound familiar: Don't get behind; take subjects outside your major; and apply your skills outside the classroom. The principles of good study, as you have seen, apply to every course, whether you are studying in humanities, science, art, language, or business.

Now that we have study skills behind us, let's look in the next chapter at survival skills of a more basic sort: where to live, who to live with, and what to live on.

Study Potpourri

SECTION

3

EXTRACURRICULAR LIFE

CHAPTER
11

PLACES AND PESOS:
That New Living Situation
& the Color of Money

Twenty-five years ago this fall, I packed up the family Ford station wagon, got in the car with my mother and grandmother who wanted to accompany me on this momentous day, and drove two hours to college. My dad was working and my grandfather was dead—otherwise, they'd have been in the car as well. I remember pulling into the "campus loop," finding the nearest parking spot next to the residence hall, and moving my possessions into a room that had all the pizzazz of a doctor's office. I was at college; I had arrived; this would be *my* place for the year. After I got my stuff into the room, I sent Mom and Nana on their way—after all, who wants to start school with a mother and grandmother in the room. But after they drove away, an eerie feeling came to take their place, a feeling that told me, "This is *not* my home." It took a while—weeks—for that feeling to leave.

One of the greatest differences between high school and college is the new living situation. Few of us have lived away from home for any length of time before we make the pilgrimage to the university. We have been away for weekends and for summer camps, and some of us have lived overseas as part of a student exchange program. But even if we were fortunate enough to have had that cross-cultural experience, we probably lived with a family. So when we head for college, we are not used to living away from a home and a family.

That new living situation brings with it a myriad of questions: Where will I live? Should I live in a dorm, an apartment, or a Greek house? Who should I live with, and how can we ever get along? How can I make this place feel like home?

Let's look at some possible answers to those questions.

Where Will I Live?

First, check out what the school offers. Write the university and ask them to send you their information on housing. Find out prices, meal plan information, the location of the residence halls in relation to the rest of the campus, deadlines for applying for rooms, and the deposit required.

Then, if possible, visit the campus for one of their orientation weekends and scope out the possibilities first hand. Talk to students you know who have gone to that school and ask them what they think of the housing available—they are sure to have strong opinions on the matter! Ask them what they dislike and like about a particular dorm, fraternity, or sorority. Then talk to some students who have lived off campus. You may want to look into apartment complexes or houses for rent. However, I'd strongly recommend that you live on campus at least the first couple years.

Obviously you'll know much more about housing *after* you've been on campus for a while than you ever will *before* you get on campus, regardless of how many people you talk to. And once you have that information, you'll be able to make better choices for the future. You'll probably live in different locations throughout your college career, so, although choosing the first place you live is an important decision, it's not a final one. You won't be trapped there for the rest of your university life if you don't want to be.

Sometimes, schools make the decision for you with their residency requirements or their frosh dorms. If that's the case, you'll only need to investigate what frosh dorm seems to be the best for you or which floor in the dorm you'd prefer.

Whether you choose to live in a frat or a dorm, an apartment or a sorority, you need to research the options, check out locations, and listen to opinions, then make a decision—knowing that you're not chained to that spot for the next four years.

To help you make your decision, I asked Sue Harris, an '88 grad, to give me the pros and cons of dorm living, apartment living, and Greek living. Having lived in all three situations during her college years, she can speak from experience. (Keep in mind that each campus is different; some of the points we make here may not be true of the living situation you select.) Here's what she concluded:

Dorm Life

Dorm life has many advantages. You live with fellow students, meals are generally provided, and you have community spaces (lounges and game rooms) that are cleaned for you. You probably live closer to campus than those living in apartments or Greek houses, so you can get to classes and extracurricular activities quickly and conveniently. Some social events are organized for you. And, finally, people in the dorms are generally quite friendly. They have a tendency to be freshmen and sophomores who are still looking for friends to hang out with. In a dorm, a sense of community prevails.

But dorm life also has its disadvantages. Because people tend to move in and out quickly, you don't usually get to choose exactly where you'll live or with whom and might end up feeling like you're playing "roommate roulette." Then there's the food, well-known for its inedibility. Room decor may be as distasteful as the food, with orange and green color schemes from the sixties, or prison concrete everywhere. It's more difficult to get away from school because it surrounds you. And finally, the dorm may not offer as many social activities as the bustling Greek houses down the street.

Apartment Life

Students usually live off campus in an apartment in order to enjoy the largest measure of freedom and autonomy. If you live off-campus, you can make your own rules for whom you will live with and how you will share responsibilities. You cook your own meals. You decide where to live and how much to spend on food and supplies. You escape the campus with its crowds and noises and enjoy a measure of privacy. And you get used to "life after college" with all its demands and responsibilities.

But if your apartment or rented house isn't surrounded by students, you may feel cut off from school, and you may find it harder to get involved in group social activities. Living off campus also means cleaning everything yourself, so if you're busy, it stays dirty. You must buy your own food, cook it, and clean up when you're done—and all that takes time from studies and socializing. In summary, you spend more time on basic living skills than you do in a fraternity, sorority, or dorm.

Greek Life

The Greek system is definitely the best at providing you with social options. That's because the houses work hard at providing more opportunities for socializing than most dorms. There is always some activity going on, and lots of people with whom to be involved. You meet people galore in the Greek system—men and women from other houses, people in the community, alumni—and you can get involved in community service. You form deep friendships because you have the continuity of the same people living with you over a couple of years. With all the people around, you have abundant opportunities for fellowship and for places to exercise your leadership skills.

You're spoiled when you live in a house; people cook for you and clean up after you. And payment for these services is simple and convenient (and sometimes less expensive than dorm payments), for you pay only one big bill at the beginning of the term and don't pay for anything else after that except personal expenses.

All these people and events can be negatives as well as positives. You may easily be overwhelmed, swallowed up in a swirl of events and people. If you're not the social type, you may find the constant round of parties tiresome. And if you *are* the social type, you may find yourself getting caught up in the party scene to the detriment of your studies. A house may be noisy, and you may get tired of switching rooms and roommates every quarter.

If the advantages of Greek life appeal to you, start looking into it as soon as possible—preferably, long before you arrive on campus. Begin with learning what you can about rush, the process used to select who will live where. Rush procedures vary from campus to campus, so check with the campus to see how rush is organized there. Some campuses also organize "Greek weekends," spring visits to the houses to get you acquainted with the Greek system. For general information about sororities, write to Panhellenic, the organization that networks the sororities. To find out about fraternities, contact the Interfraternity Council. But the best way to learn about the Greek system is to talk to students who are involved or alumni who know the current situation.

Sue has some good advice for anyone thinking of joining a sorority or fraternity:

a. Don't be afraid to go through rush even if you don't know anybody at the school or in the area. Rush is a great time to meet people and find out interesting tidbits about your campus and the surrounding area, especially the fun places like unusual stores and places to hang out.

b. Remember there are a number of houses.

There *is* a place for you if you want to rush, but you have to keep an open mind as you go through the process.

c. As you go through rush, be yourself; don't try to project a certain image. Then you are more likely to find a house where *you* feel the most comfortable. At a university, people like to rank the houses and come up with the "best house." Everyone has an opinion of which house that is—parents, friends, alumni, everybody will give you their opinion. But the truth is there is no "best house" in the university. There is simply the "best house for you."

How Do I Live with This Roommate?

Relationships always have great potential for joy and for sorrow, and relationships in a living situation are no different. Sometimes you can choose your own roommate. Many times you can't. If you move into a fraternity or sorority, roommates are usually assigned (and there may be more than one, further complicating the situation). And if you're attending a college where you know no one else, you'll have a roommate assigned out of necessity. So that's how your living situation most likely will begin. You'll be rooming with someone you probably don't know.

Mark Hogendobler says, "I had a roommate who was radically different from me. When I applied for housing, I didn't even think of requesting a Christian roommate, but I should have because the environment was foreign enough as it was. I didn't need to deal with all the political, religious, interpersonal, girlfriend problems that my roommate brought with him. I felt at times like a caged animal surrounded by malicious keepers who jabbed their pointed, red-hot spears at me whenever the opportunity arose. I also happened to draw a floor of sophomores, most of whom were friends of each other and who had the same, atheistic attitudes about things. I was a naive Christian southerner as out of place as Ghandi at a Ku Klux Klan rally. I survived, but I know all too well what it is like to be the one against many."

That's a tough way to begin a university experience. Fortunately, it's not typical. But a match like Mark's can happen. Usually the people in charge of housing do their best in matching people, but none of these matches will have been made in heaven—all will have been made in some administrative place, and you may not like the match. But believe me, roommate selections you have made yourself are not sure

winners either. It's amazing how living with someone changes your previous perceptions of that individual! The best of friends may become the worst of enemies after they live together.

How do you live with this person you may or may not have selected?

Sometime in the first few weeks of school you need to set up some ground rules for your room or house and then stick to those rules. For example, you may draw up a list of cleaning duties that you trade off every week. Agree that no members of the opposite sex will stay overnight; set up quiet hours. Set guidelines that are not too numerous and ones with which you can both generally agree. You may not be in perfect agreement on each point, so compromise where you can, making a set of ground rules with which you're both relatively satisfied. If you can't compromise on rules, you may want to get your resident advisor, house advisor, or another person who can act as a mediator and help resolve the conflicts. If it's absolutely impossible to work things out, you may be able to switch roommates if you act quickly. But hang in there. There is probably a solution to your problems if you're both open and honest about the situation.

When you want to ask your roommate to change, try to keep your complaints about your roommate impersonal, and try to be tactful in your requests for change. For instance, "I need a little more closet space" is much more tactful than "You're hogging all the closet space with your mess." Do not say anything to deliberately antagonize your roommate; you will only worsen the situation. Instead, make your requests sound reasonable and easy to comply with.

Remember: One of the great educational experiences of college is learning how to live with someone besides a family member. Mark suggests, "To get along with a roommate, consider him or her your personal project, as if God had put you there for the explicit purpose of demonstrating his love for that person. And know that if you decide to live with a friend, nothing strains a friendship as much as freshman year together."

In my four years in college, I lived in three different locations on campus with five different roommates.

I'm still in touch with four of the roommates, and one I haven't heard from since he left college. But I'll remember my living situations, the camaraderie in the residence halls, the bull sessions on the floors, probably more than I will remember any other aspect of college life.

How Do I Settle In?

When you start college, allow yourself some time to adjust. After forty-three years of living, I still find that it takes a while to feel comfortable in a new situation. There is no substitute for time in making yourself comfortable, so give yourself some, knowing that you will feel better later. For now, it's okay to feel homesick, lonely, left out. But remember that, even though it may seem like everyone else knows everyone, most people probably feel lonely like you—so reach out to them.

It helps, too, to make your new surroundings correspond to your tastes as much as possible. There will be some things, of course, that you can do nothing about—the view from the window, the size of the rooms, and so on. But do what you can. Put up some favorite posters, or pictures of friends or family. Set up your stereo, or find the local radio stations that play *your* kind of music. Add accents in your favorite colors—throw rugs, bedspreads, flowers, whatever. Even in many college dorms, you have some options: rearranging the beds and desks, bringing in a small refrigerator, and so on. It may be only an institutional cubicle—but it can be *your* cubicle.

The Color of Money

One of your major discoveries in college will likely be that money is a precious and limited commodity. In college you have to begin to think of ways to earn, budget, and conserve money. For that purpose, here are a few suggestions concerning money.

1. *Assess your costs and available resources.* Sit down with the college catalog and determine what college will cost you in tuition, fees, room, and board. Those prices are fairly fixed and can be determined easily. Next, assess the more difficult items: cost of books, social activities, incidentals (like your hourly can of Diet Coke), gas for your car, and transportation to and from your home. Then add a little slush fund because you'll probably underestimate.

Now look at your resources: money in the bank, scholarships, student loans, and parental help. Where does this assessment leave you? If you're like most students, you'll probably end up in the hole or near bankruptcy. So start looking for places where you can cut back. Or add some resources; work during Christmas break instead of hitchhiking to Ft. Lauderdale.

2. *If necessary, get a part-time job.* Another way to increase your resources is simply to get a part-time job. There are numerous jobs available at the university, and many of these jobs can be scheduled around your course load. Off-campus jobs also exist. But beware of working too many hours especially your first quarter or semester. Also, don't get so caught up in making extra spending money that you cheat yourself on the college experience. I had several jobs during my four years at college; I worked as a recreation director for kids at an army base, a youth director in a church, a lifeguard, and a dock boy at a marina. But I made sure I could still enjoy college.

3. *Build a budget and stick to it.* College is a great place to learn about budgeting, and what you learn in college will "profit" you the rest of your life. As you budget, save a bit for a rainy day. And don't forget to set aside a tithe on what you make as well. If you handle your money as a gift from God, he will bless this aspect of your life too, giving you the resources you need for your college expenses.

Places and pesos—both are part of the total college education. Now we'll look in the next chapter at how to deal with people and pressure.

CHAPTER

12

PEOPLE AND
PRESSURE:
Saying Yes and No

College is one of the best places to make friends and sustain friendships. College provides so many great "excuses" to meet casually.

"Let's study together."

"Let's take a break and get some coffee."

"Let's get away from campus for an hour."

"Let's go down to the intramural building and shoot some hoops."

Social opportunities abound.

College also provides intense times of getting to know each other intimately, one on one. After living with your roommate day after day, you get to know that person fairly well—in some cases, too well! Living away from home means that you and your friends rely on each other more for moral support. And if a friendship with the opposite sex blooms into romance, you will grow close to that person also.

Knowing about all the friendship possibilities, you may want some tips on how to develop and maintain good relationships. Here are a few suggestions.

Saying "Yes" to Friends

1. *Make the development and maintenance of friendships a high priority in your life.* Realize that putting a priority on friendships will require an investment of time and energy. Sue Jernberg, now a grad student, says, "When I was a sophomore in college, I made a decision affecting my schooling, which I have never regretted. I decided that, although I could expend 100 percent of my effort on studies and come away with a bunch of very high grades in classes, I would be missing out. It was more worthwhile to me to delegate a bit less time to school in order to be more involved in ministry, in building a couple of important friendships, and in spending time with my family. I had learned an important lesson. You receive back what you pay out both in school and in other areas. Invest in academics and you get grades. Invest in relationships and you develop friendships."

2. *Take the initiative: Go where people are.* If you're new on a campus, get involved. If you join a fraternity or sorority, you'll immediately be surrounded with people. If you're in a dorm, make sure you attend a dorm meeting or function. Sign up for an intramural team. Join a special interest club. Be open to people who may be different from the gang you hung out with in high school—expand your horizons. And, if you have a choice, live on campus. That's the quickest way to get involved.

If you can't live on campus, if you are a commuter, you will have to possess extra initiative. Commuter students have a unique problem in making friendships and being part of the social life on campus. Often they stick with friends from high school if they have trouble forming new friendships. But if you are a commuter, make an effort to break out of your high school group. Join a campus fellowship group. Take part in extracurricular activities—choir, intramurals, student government, newspaper, radio station, or drama troupe. And spend as much time as possible on campus, studying in the library and eating in the student union. All these places and activities provide opportunities for meeting people if you take advantage of them. And, if possible, live on campus at least one quarter of your college career. It's worth it.

3. *Be yourself.* Don't be a hypocrite or try to cover up who you are and where you came from. You won't need to fake it to get people to like you. In the long run, you want to be accepted for who you are, so let people get to know the real you.

4. *Don't compromise your morals as you begin friendships.* Part of being yourself is maintaining your integrity even if you feel so lonely that you're tempted to adjust your standards in order to be accepted. We'll talk about moral choices later in the chapter, but for now you should know that if you compromise your morals to gain some friendships, you'll regret your choice later. Think of a friendship as a long-term investment, not a quick fix. It may take longer to find and pursue friendships with certain people, but a good friendship that comes later is worth much more than a bad friendship right now.

5. *Be a good listener.* Often the key to developing a friendship is to be a good listener. So listen—and as you listen, concentrate, giving your friend your full attention. Then, knowing that you really care, your friend will open up to you even more.

Of course, a good friend will allow you the chance to talk too. A good friendship is always a healthy balance between talking and listening; if you always talk, you'll never get to know your friend, and if you always listen, your friend will never get to know you. So share your thoughts, and you'll not only build your friendship but also help each other out.

6. *Stay in touch with off-campus friends and family.* Let your old friends know that you haven't forgotten them in all the excitement of college and that their friendship means a lot to you. Send your friends a simple card or a long letter. You may not get as much return mail as you want but don't let that discourage you—some people just aren't writers. Let those friends know when you'll be back in town so that they can plan on spending some time with you.

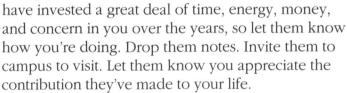

Also be sure to keep in regular contact with your family. They have invested a great deal of time, energy, money, and concern in you over the years, so let them know how you're doing. Drop them notes. Invite them to campus to visit. Let them know you appreciate the contribution they've made to your life.

7. *Realize that you can't be a close friend to everyone.* You probably won't be able to maintain all your past friendships at the same level of closeness you have now with college friends. Mark Hogendobler says, "Appreciate friendships while they last and don't be frustrated or discouraged when friendships fade slowly because of changes in location or changes of interest. There is no reason to feel guilty and insist that all your friendships will last forever. Appreciate them while they are there and don't force a friendship to continue at the same intensity when situations change. Consider each relationship, whether long- or short-

157 People and Pressures

term, as another great opportunity provided you by God to love and be loved, to learn and to teach. And, remember, if these friends are Christians, you'll be able to spend all   eternity together."

8. *Broaden your friendships.* Jim Francese, who was deeply immersed in the sciences, says, "It's important to build relationships with your lab partners and people you do homework with. But I feel it is also desirable to maintain relationships with people in other majors who have other interests. This can be difficult, for as we progress through college, the classes get specialized and contain fewer students. We spend many, many hours with people within our own major area of specialization. It is a natural tendency to think of these people first when we want to go out with someone or when we need a new roommate. But part of the college education is a social education, and getting to know a variety of people enhances this education."

To meet people from diverse backgrounds and from different parts of the country, Jim lived in a fraternity for three years at Cornell. Like Jim, you can get to know people in your house or dorm. You can also deliberately take classes in other majors to meet students outside your field. Finally, you can get involved in a campus fellowship group. Besides the primary purpose of glorifying God and meeting spiritual needs, the group provides an opportunity for students to get to know one another.

9. *Date—don't be "just friends" with everyone.* Many of the principles outlined above are appropriate in developing relationships with members of the opposite sex. But, of course, there's more to a relationship once it turns romantic. Sometimes, romantic relationships begin with a good friendship. But at other times, romance begins with pursuit and pursuit begins with a date.

If you are reluctant to date, date anyhow. Choose your dates carefully, but don't have such a long list of criteria that no one qualifies. As you think about dating someone more than once, the criteria become more important because the longer you date, the greater the chance to become romantically involved and the more romantically involved you become, the closer you come to marriage. So look for someone who has a common faith in Jesus Christ, who shares your dreams and goals, and who has some interests in common with you (but not all interests—that would be boring). And date many people. The more you date, the more comfortable you'll feel in dating, the more people you'll get to know, and the better idea you'll have of what kind of person you want to marry.

At any rate, date.

Saying No to Pressures

With friends and groups and crowds come certain pressures that are particularly prominent in the college scene. Talking about relationships would not be complete without talking about the pressures these relationships bring with them, specifically the "Big Three" pressures of the university setting—alcohol, sex, and drugs.

As a person who spends most of his time with college students, I am aware of the pervasive pressures of the Big Three. Alcohol is rampant on our campus.

Everyone can drink and many do. Alcohol is freely dispersed at the vast majority of social functions, and memorabilia, beer in particular, proliferates in the shape of posters, mugs, and T-shirts. Drugs also are available, although the number of students doing drugs is less than those engaged in moderate-to-heavy drinking. Finally, our campus abounds in sexual temptation, usually beginning with lust. When I surveyed college students at a fellowship group about their greatest temptations, sex and lust easily topped the list.

The pressures of the world are great, and they are multiplied in college. The pressures to participate is greater when "everyone is doing it" (or so it seems). And, let's be honest, there is a momentary high, a buzz, a pleasurable sensation with all three of the temptation areas.

Seldom does anyone begin to participate in something potentially harmful with the idea that he will become addicted and watch his life destroyed, but social drinking, recreational drug taking, and casual sex can lead to disaster.

Saying no takes guts, requiring an independence that is exciting at times and lonely at others. Saying no is difficult and requires some special helps. Before we look more specifically at the three pressures, let's look at the specific helps that God's Word gives us for dealing with these pressures.

1 Corinthians 3:16 asks us, "Don't you know that you yourselves are God's temple and that God's Spirit lives in you?"

Ephesians 5:3 adds, "But among you there must not be even a hint of sexual immorality, or of any kind of impurity, or of greed, because these are improper for God's holy people."

Then in 1 Peter 2:11, these words are given: "Dear friends, I urge you, as aliens and strangers in the world, to abstain from sinful desires, which war against your soul. Live such good lives among the pagans that, though they accuse you of doing wrong, they may see your good deeds and glorify God on the day he visits us." These verses tell us that God has set a standard for our behavior, a standard that will make it necessary for us to sometimes say no.

These verses show us that we say no to wrong because we are God's temple and he dwells within us. When we say yes to wrong, we are attaching God to that evil. We are inviting the Creator and Lord of all to muck around with us in wrongdoing. That's incomprehensible, isn't it?

These verses also tell us that for God's people, impurity, immorality, and greed are improper. These characteristics are inconsistent with the Christian life, and they are also as incompatible as oil and water. Such actions are improper not only because they're wrong but also because they're hurtful. God says no because he wants what's best for us, not because he's a cosmic killjoy trying to stamp out our fun. He wants us to be sexually happy, so he designed the sacrament of marriage. He wants us to live life on a high but intoxicated us with his Holy Spirit, not with worldly spirits. (When you think about it, it's quite interesting that alcohol is often called "spirits"!)

And finally, by walking with God, we serve as a witness to the world. We have a responsibility to those watching us to live a life that glorifies God. Part of our maturing is accepting that responsibility.

We need to remember that God blesses obedience and punishes disobedience. The Bible is full of promises to those who are faithful. When students step away from wrong and head down the road labeled "right," God blesses them. Trust God to honor your obedience and reward you with abundant life, a life that is full and complete without the addictions of the Big Three. But the converse is also true: God punishes the disobedient. Sometimes God punishes our disobedience simply by allowing us to "reap what we sow"— to face the consequences of our actions. For sin *does* have its consequences, now and eternally.

You can prevent yourself from falling if you say no quickly, at the first time temptation presents itself. Saying no early on will help you establish your standards and reputation, and the pressure to conform will not be as great. People will recognize your stance and back off a bit. Some may still try to make you fall, but the pressure won't be as great if your standards are set.

Believe it or not, living morally is just as fun and exciting as living your life in the grip of the Big Three. Enjoy the company of a group that makes the right thing the popular thing, and you'll find that, because the pressures and consequences of the sex, alcohol, drugs are missing, your fun will be less tainted with messy complications.

Now that we've established some general principles for saying no, let's look at some specific hints for dealing with alcohol, drugs, and sex.

Dealing with Alcohol

If you already are drinking, you should stop and ask yourself some questions. First ask: "Why do I drink?" Do you drink to get a buzz, release tension, fit in, rebel against Christianity, or cool yourself down after a hot day? Some of your answers to these questions may give you a clue to your drinking habits and how acceptable to God they are.

Then ask: "How do I act when I drink?" Sometimes alcohol makes certain people dangerously violent, or, in another vein, dangerously compliant to sexual temptations. Some people become more daring, open, and rowdy, saying and doing things they wish later hadn't been said and done. Since we all have to live with what we do, you may want to consider some of the consequences of inappropriate behavior. If you can't handle what alcohol does to you, stay away from it.

The previous question ties in closely to this one: "Do I know my drinking limits?" If you behave badly under certain amounts of alcohol, limit how much you drink. And if you have alcoholic tendencies, if you feel yourself *needing* a drink, if you get smashed every weekend, or if you show any other signs of addiction, stop drinking immediately and get help. Finally, if your family has a history of addiction, never start drinking— or quit drinking *now*.

The last question you should ask yourself is: "How are others affected by my drinking?" The Bible tells us not to be a stumbling stone to our brothers and sisters in the Lord. It can be an ugly testimony to new believers to see Christians returning to the world's system to find happiness and fulfillment. As a person who wants to disciple and lead others, you want new believers to learn from your actions as well as your words.

For some, your answers to these questions will lead you to modify your drinking habits so that you use alcohol only in small amounts and only at carefully prescribed times. But others will want or need to choose the route of total abstention. Rod Handley says, "For me, it is much easier to totally abstain from alcohol because it removes the appearance of evil and sets up a standard for fellow Christians and non-Christians to observe. Because I have maintained this consistency, I have seen people respect my views and have found people who are encouraged by my example. Through discussions with people, I have found that many do not enjoy the drinking scene at all but drink because they feel so much pressure to fit in. Unless you take a strong stance against drinking, people will really pressure you to conform. But as you say no, you will be encouraged that people can accept you even when you don't drink. What it really comes down to is that many people push others to drink so they won't feel so bad about drinking themselves."

Dealing with drugs

My advice in this section is short, sweet, and simple: Don't even touch drugs. Avoid them like the plague they are. Drugs are expensive, illegal, and lethal. They can deform and damage your offspring, ruin your brain cells, land you in jail, and enslave you to a life of addiction, secrecy, and subterfuge. No momentary high can be worth the high price paid in a life ruined by drugs.

Dealing with Sex

Unless you are living in a monastery, you'll probably find it harder to say no to sexual temptations than to the temptation to take drugs. I'm sure you've heard the argument, "After all, sex is a natural drive; it deserves to be fulfilled." But remember, when people give you that argument, that premarital and extra-marital sex are not part of God's plan. God designed sex to be a beautiful act, holy, healthy, healing, loving, and exciting—if kept within marriage. Deal with sex according to God's guidelines, and you will never have to carry around the burden of regret. But if you violate God's intentions for sex, problems and hurts will result.

What are the injuries that result from premarital and extra-marital sex? First there is the psychological hurt. When two people become intimately involved in a sexual relationship, a strong emotional and psychological bond develops, even if the couple insists that it is just "casual" sex. If and when a break-up occurs, scars result. As responsible people, we must be concerned for the other person in the relationship. Not only do we not want to be scarred, we don't want to inflict scars on others.

Besides psychological hurts, there may also be physical hurts. Unwanted pregnancy, venereal disease, and now AIDS threaten those who dabble casually in sexual relationships.

A simple way to avoid these hurts and remove yourself from sexual temptation is to avoid the trouble spots, like the backseat of your car, or your room when your roommate is away. If you choose the proper location for your date, you can avoid a lot of trouble. For example, very few people make love while sitting in a crowded coffee shop! If you've been very tempted, agree with your boyfriend or girlfriend to avoid the trouble spots.

Sometimes you will not only have to avoid places but people too. If you hang around with a crowd who encourages casual sex, they may tempt you to change your standards. Or your boyfriend or girlfriend may be one of the people pressuring you to give in to sexual temptation. If so, you may have to break up with that person, fleeing from the temptation. Remember, it's better to look like a coward and run than to look like a hero and fail.

People can be both the joys of your college life and a part of the pressures of college life depending on how you deal with them. But you have two simple words for coping with the pressures of college: "Yes" and "No." Learn how and when to use these words, and you'll be well on your way to surviving college.

CHAPTER

13

HUMILITY 101:
*Loving Yourself in the
Midst of Imperfection*

In the 1988 Superbowl, in front of a worldwide television audience of one hundred *million* people, cornerback Barry Wilburn of the Washington Redskins was burned on a pass play by Denver's Ricky Nattiel and John Elway. One of my favorite "professional journals," *Sports Illustrated*, said of the play: "Wilburn clawed desperately at Ricky Nattiel's ankles as the Bronco Amigo caught the pass and scored the game's first touchdown. The world seemed to explode in Wilburn's ears as he looked up at the blue California sky above Jack Murphy Stadium. He was thinking, 'Why me?' All-pro Darrell Green, the Redskins other corner, came over to Wilburn as 200 million eyes watched Denver's wild celebration. 'Forget it, Barry,' said Green. 'Don't worry about that. You know the rule.'"

The rule for the Washington Redskins is as applicable for students as it is for National Football League cornerbacks who display their mistakes and miscues before millions: "Anybody can be great when it's easy. But when you're down, that's when the great corner in you has to step up and say, 'Challenge me again.' The first rule: It's how you come back from being beaten that matters."

One of the most difficult pills to swallow in college is that there are lots of people who are just as smart, athletic, attractive, and humorous as you. And there are some who are much more so.

A second nearly indigestible pill is that failure is very possible and quite probable in college. You may fail in a relationship, you may fail in a class, you most likely will fail meeting a personal expectation. You may think of yourself as able to handle life and then feel like a failure when you find yourself stressed, burned out, and ill. You will disappoint yourself and will probably disappoint friends and family.

So one thing you're certain to have in common with cornerback Barry Wilburn is that sooner or later, you'll be beaten and you'll have to remember the rule: It's how you come back from being beaten that matters. That rule is only one of many lessons learned in Humility 101, a required course in the curriculum that no one escapes.

Going through this course will make you wonder: How do you love yourself and maintain a semblance of self-confidence when you've failed? Here are some principles I myself learned in Humility 101 that have helped me, and hopefully these pointers will help you as well.

1. *Forgive yourself.* If your failure is related to sin or is the result of a stupid mistake, forgive yourself and confess your sin to the Lord. Know that God will forgive you, as promised in 1 John 1:9: "If we confess our sins, he is faithful and just and will forgive us our sins and purify us from all unrighteousness."

If God has forgiven you, you need to forgive yourself. Forgiving yourself may be difficult. You may need to say aloud, "I forgive me," before the concept will sink in. Or you may need to say those words in front of your friend so that he or she can be a witness that you've forgiven yourself.

Other people may have been involved in your failure. If so, after you've confessed your sin, received God's forgiveness, and forgiven yourself, you will have to go to the person you've hurt, ask their forgiveness and make restitution if necessary.

But with some failures only you are hurt. Don't ignore that hurt, hoping it will go away. Confess it, forgive it, take it to the Lord. He knows when you've failed and will be with you, one on one, through the time of hurt and humiliation.

2. *Begin anew.* I like fresh starts; in fact, I'm almost a fresh start fanatic. To me, every day is a *new* day, a time for beginnings. So is every week, every month, every semester, every year. I love fresh starts and new beginnings, because if God has cleansed us, purified us, and removed our sins from us as far as the east is from the west (Psalm 103:12), then he has obviously gifted us with a new day. All we have to do is accept that new day; then begin anew.

3. *Don't draw generalizations.* For instance, if you should fail a test, don't come to this conclusion: "I guess I'm just too dumb for college. I'll never succeed. I might as well drop out now and save myself some time, money, and headaches." Generalizations are paralyzing. So you failed—I know lots of students who have failed one test in a course. I also know of students who have failed a course or dropped it on the last possible day. But if you fail, don't draw generalizations. Instead, analyze what happened, as you will learn to do in the next point.

4. *Learn from your mistakes.* As I mentioned previously, analyze what happens if you fail, by asking and answering some questions. If you failed a test, did you study hard? If the answer is yes, did you study well? Did you study with the right people? Analyze the test score. Where did you make your mistakes? Do you understand the best way to take tests (see chapter 7)? Whatever you do, don't draw the generalization that you're dumb and should be bailing out.

To take another example, if a relationship fails, don't say, "Well, I guess I just don't have the personality to sustain a relationship." Unless you're extremely strange, that's probably the wrong conclusion to make. But there might be something from the ending of this relationship that you can learn before beginning a new one. It may be a truism, but we usually do learn more from failure than we do from success.

5. *Accept your weaknesses as well as your strengths.* I learned in college that I did not have the most brilliant scientific mind and re-learned that I was not the most gifted person in foreign languages. I learned that there were guys who were quicker than I on the basketball court. I could accept that. But I also learned that, with hard work, I could improve in areas where I was weak. That old prayer, "God grant me the courage to change the things I can, the serenity to accept the things I can't, and the wisdom to know the difference," is a great prayer for us to say.

As you go through college, sometimes you will be dramatically reminded of your strengths and sometimes painfully reminded of your weaknesses. You may flunk out of the basic, required math course. But you may score high in an upper level history course. Whether you fail or succeed, take advantage of these incidents, using them as signposts steering you away from one path of life and into another.

6. *Don't forget who loves you.* God loves you. The Bible is full of references to that fact. A familiar one is John 3:16: "For God so loved the world that he gave his one and only Son, that whoever believes in him shall not perish but have eternal life." God loved *you* so much that he died for you. To remind myself of God's love, sometimes I substitute my name for "the world": "For God so loved Denny Rydberg..." That, to me, is mind-boggling!

But Christ *did* die for me and for you, and when we have a relationship with Christ, nothing can separate us from his love. Romans 8:38-39 reads, "For I am convinced that neither death nor life, neither angels nor demons, neither the present nor the future, nor any powers, neither height nor depth, nor anything else in all creation, will be able to separate us from the love of God that is in Christ Jesus our Lord."

We are God's children and he's crazy about us. He loves us unconditionally and completely. Even when others have rejected us, God will never reject us or stop loving us no matter what we do. God is not in love with our sinful actions, but he continues to love *us*.

In the midst of failure, also remind yourself that there are *people* in the world who care about you and will stand by you. I went through my greatest devastating personal failure over ten years ago. It was my fault, my sin alone. But in the midst of the mess I created, many (not all) friends remained. The same will be true for you. Besides family members, you can turn to your friends, your fellowship group, or your church for support.

7. *Don't run away from your support group.* In order to receive love and support, you need to seek help. But sometimes when you fail, you have an intense desire to hide out. You don't want to face people who know what you've done because you fear condemnation and rejection. But don't run away. This time of trouble is the time when the body of Christ needs to stick together. You need their support, and they need to learn to deal with you in love and forgiveness.

This year, one of the guys who attended our fellowship group was arrested for a serious crime. He was drunk at the time and couldn't remember all the details. During the spring, he continued to come to our group meetings even though the cloud over his head darkened as more evidence emerged. I think the group was what helped hold him together. No one (that I know of) ostracized him. On the other hand, no one rationalized or minimized the crime either. People reserved judgment on his guilt, knowing he was innocent until proven guilty, and even in his guilt they were willing to stick with him.

But this summer as the final stages of the trial proceeded and as the trial began, the guy backed off from the support group. I don't think he's doing very well right now. He needs the support, the constant nurture of a group who knows and loves him. People are still praying for him and trying to reach out to him, but he's avoiding their help.

Don't be like this guy; don't run away from your

Humility 101

group even if the disaster is of epic proportions. You will need their support and love so that you do not grow bitter and fall further into sin.

8. *Accept God's pruning in your life.* The Bible says that those whom God loves, he prunes so that they will be even more fruitful (John 15:2). Rod Handley knows firsthand about the pruning process. He grew up in a fruit-growing region, and his dad, an orchardist, taught Rod how to prune trees. This is what Rod said of his pruning lesson: "The first year I pruned, I just couldn't figure out why we were cutting down all those limbs. I thought we were losing a fortune in money by killing those branches. Later I discovered that the pruning process actually caused a greater crop of apples to grow. The pruning helped balance the tree, aided in maintaining appropriate water levels to let the tree survive, created space in the tree, and enhanced the color and growth of the apples. Later, after examining other orchards where pruning had not occurred, I saw trees with fewer apples that were also of poorer quality. The pruning process may seem difficult, but it prepares for a greater crop in the future. In the same way that my father pruned the trees,

God prunes us. An expert in his field, God will shape and prune you to bear quantities of high-quality fruit."

Now I don't believe that God personally designs all the tough experiences we encounter. I don't think God loves illness or failure. But, as Sovereign Lord, he allows the results of sin in the world to hit both Christians and non-Christians alike. Biblical language says that "the rain falls on both the just and the unjust." Good people aren't immune. Christian people aren't immune. (And sometimes there is a big difference between Christian people and good people. Not all good people are Christians. Sadly, not all Christians are good people.) But God uses all experiences and events for good in our lives. As Romans 8:28 says, "We know that in all things God works for the good of those who love him, who have been called according to his purpose." God doesn't waste an experience.

Pete Shimer, a softball-playing buddy of mine, says that through a broken relationship that hurt him deeply he learned compassion and the importance of the community of believers. Up to that point in his life, Pete had been on a roll. Success came easily to him. And with success had come very little understanding for those who were hurting. His own failure taught him some important lessons.

Like Pete, I learned important lessons from my failures. In high school, I started two years on the varsity basketball team. I had never ridden the bench in basketball—never. Then in my frosh year of college, I learned what it meant to ride the pines, to get into the game on the whim of the coach and to have to produce immediately. Sometimes I did well, sometimes I didn't. It was tough. But I can identify now with both starters and with guys on the bench. Through my failures God has probably taught me more than he taught through my successes.

9. *Laugh at yourself.* It's usually easier to laugh after the fact, when the pain of failure has lessened. But laugh as soon as possible, so that others will laugh *with* you. A sense of humor helps you to face your failures, putting them into proper perspective. And a sense of humor helps you learn from your mistakes.

As you face failures and mistakes, remember the advice I gave for dealing with those mistakes, and above all, remember God's love for you even when you fail. With that kind of support behind you, you'll even pass Humility 101—the universal course—with great grades.

CHAPTER 14

A SPECIAL KIND OF SURVIVAL
The Christian University

Up to this point in the book, we have concentrated on survival and success in the university arena in general. What has been written could apply to any institution of higher learning and to any college student. But there is a unique university situation that needs its own chapter—the Christian university.

I graduated from a Christian college after investing all four years there. I've also spent time in the secular university program. I took a T.A. position at a state school for one quarter before deciding that behavioral psychology wasn't for me. And I've spent the last five years of my life ministering to students on secular campuses.

Brent Plate is a friend of mine who knows about the dual worlds of secular and Christian higher education. Last fall, he transferred from a state university in California to a Christian university in Seattle. Here's what he told me about the move: "What I feared most about going to a Christian school was always that I would get too comfortable and my faith would not be so sharp. I knew people coming out of Christian colleges who had no idea of what goes on in the world. Sure, they had a good deal of knowledge on what it meant to be a Christian, but they didn't know what a Christian does. The Christian college too often becomes a fortress—whether or not it is a mighty fortress I do not know—a place shut out from the rest of the world. Christians are there operating in a vacuum; the propositional truth is there but not the experiential because there is no 'testing of the faith.' I have heard some Christian colleges described as 'Spiritual Disneylands.'"

I think Brent has defined the problem well.

Sometimes the Christian college can be so heavenly-minded that it's no earthly good. It may be a spiritual cocoon, so removed from life that you are ill-equipped to move into the world. So before you choose to attend a Christian college, you should ask yourself questions

like these: What are the advantages and disadvantages of attending a Christian university? Are the advantages worth it? Can the disadvantages be overcome to the point where it definitely is a wise decision to attend? How can a person survive at good old "Blest Be the Tie that Binds" University?

Advantages of the Christian University

1. *Christian professors integrate their faith with their field of study.* Having Christian professors is a tremendous advantage, for you learn from people who have been "thinking Christianly" about life and academics for years. Your professors pass on their wisdom and expertise, guiding you as you establish your own worldview.

2. *If the school encourages you to ask questions, it provides a great environment in which to grow.* Thomas Merton said, "I think a man is known better by his questions than his answers." College is the time to start wrestling with those questions, questions about upbringing, faith, culture, philosophy, and theology.

The Christian college can be a near-perfect place to ask questions because, first of all, you have thoughtful Christians on the faculty and staff who have dealt with these questions for years and have a commitment to the spiritual development of the students. And secondly, on Christian campuses, students themselves are concerned with their spiritual lives. I have noticed on a secular campus that although many students say they believe in the existence of God and some even give lip service to the fact that Jesus deserves respect, they don't talk about God and act as if Jesus had never been born. On a Christian campus, students are more likely to talk about their faith.

As I reflect on my Christian college days, I know that I could and did ask difficult questions and that my beliefs were shaken to the core and modified somewhat by my answers. A course in abnormal psychology was the catalyst for me. My Christian professor, who was young and enthusiastic, didn't water down the subject or the inherent problems that I saw, and I was faced with the age-old question of how a loving God could allow terrible psychological abnormalities. I was forced to deal with the existence of evil, to dig into apologetics, to rebuild my faith on a more solid theological foundation. With other students, too, faith issues were a topic of conversation. We talked about Jesus. We acted like he existed. And we worked on our faith.

3. *A Christian school provides a good setting for a moratorium.* Some educators have developed the idea of "college as a moratorium." Moratorium means "an authorized period of delay in the performance of a legal obligation or the payment of a debt." It also means "a waiting period set by an authority, a suspension of activity." The idea for college as a moratorium means that students should be encouraged to take a break from the normal demands of life to concentrate on building a foundation for the future. A Christian college provides a special sort of moratorium, sheltering a person from even more of the pressures of life— increased secularization, intensified temptation, and so on.

From my own experience, I know that a Christian school won't shield you from all temptations. My faith was tested pragmatically. I was tempted sexually just as I would be on a secular campus. However, drugs and alcohol were not big issues for me, nor did I have to battle a secular mindset every minute like Christians often do on a state campus. So college was a bit like summer camp, for I was set apart with like-minded people.

I must admit regretfully that my college did seem like a cocoon at times. I went to campus in the mid-sixties when a revolution was brewing on other campuses. The Vietnam War was heating up, and the drug culture, hippies, and free sex made their way onto most campuses. But somehow the winds of ferment blew by our campus. I'm sorry I wasn't more perceptive about the world, and I'm sorry I missed what I did. That would have been a great time to be a Christian struggling with issues and sharing faith on a secular campus.

I did have to face the struggles of finances, relationships, and doing right when it was easier to do wrong, but my college was somewhat of a moratorium.

It was a time when I could be more exposed to a Christian perspective before being more fully exposed to the secular world.

Moratorium may be a plus or it may be a minus. But for now I'll put it on the advantage side.

4. *Smaller classes, more personal attention, professors who can concentrate more on teaching and less on publishing are the norm in the Christian college.* Part of the reason is that Christian schools are typically smaller in size. But part of the reason is design. Undergraduates seem to be valued more highly at a Christian school and professors are not judged so much on what they write as how they teach and relate to students. (But, beware, you can run into as many academic duds at a Christian school as you can at a state school. And there are some outstanding professors in the bigger universities who teach brilliantly and who care about the students.)

5. *Prayer is emphasized.* In some classes, the hour begins with prayer. A prayerful atmosphere is good for study, for concentration, for questioning, for relating.

6. *Opportunities abound to hear outstanding Christian speakers.* Christian colleges often bring Christian speakers to campus for chapels and special assemblies. But you have to go to chapel to hear them—and not everyone does. In fact, I've detected a trend among Christian college students to skip the chapels. I suggest you don't. I made it a point in college to go to chapels, and I profited from them. I heard speakers I would never have heard if I hadn't invested the time. Sure, there were days when I wasted my time, but there were also days when I was greatly enriched by the good speakers. So I encourage you to attend.

The Disadvantages of the Christian University

1. *You can lose your evangelistic edge.* I didn't have a great evangelistic edge to start with, but when I got to school I lost what little edge I had. Because most of the students on my campus were Christians or had heard the Gospel, I got the subtle impression that the wider world had heard the message and didn't want it either. When the table overflows with food, no one has to ask for more or go to the pantry, and I think I got the mistaken impression that people weren't hungry for the Gospel. What a poor impression! When I got out of the Christian college setting and into the wider world, I discovered that God has built a hunger into many people who are waiting to hear a clear presentation of the good news.

2. *A Christian college is a great place to rebel against your faith.* When your faith isn't being tested every day and when the evangelistic edge is gone, spiritual apathy tends to set in. When that happens, people can become cynical about their faith. That's one form of rebellion.

Another form of rebellion is active rebellion. Christian schools have more rules and regulations than secular schools. People "under the law" have been rebelling against the law for years, and more laws simply provide more ways to rebel. In addition, some of the students have felt forced by their parents to attend a Christian college, and rebelling becomes a way for them to get back at their parents.

3. *You can easily develop the "us vs. them" mentality.* When I was in college, we distrusted the folks at the big state school across town. We didn't want *their* guys taking out *our* girls. We also developed an "us vs. them" mentality when it came to Christians and non-Christians. We were compassionate, thoughtful, and committed—or so we thought. And those virtues, we assumed, didn't exist in "them." That sort of rotten attitude—an attitude of superiority—is not what you want to develop in college.

4. *You can get out of touch.* A Christian college, while providing a moratorium, can provide *too much* of a moratorium. You can quickly get out of touch. You may forget how to relate to non-Christians. And you may forget how to live *in* the world but not *of* it.

5. *You have fewer classes and extracurricular classes from which to choose.* If you want to work for a sophisticated school newspaper, or if you want to specialize in ballet, a small Christian college is probably not for you. While Christian colleges try to offer a little of everything, they often do not have the finances or facilities to support specialized classes or special activities. That's just the nature of a big school compared to a small one.

6. *Christian colleges are usually more expensive*

to attend. Not only does a Christian college usually cost more, but often it may not have the scholarships, athletic funds, or grants that a state university or heavily endowed larger private school might.

Surviving at the Christian University

Here are four suggestions for survival.

1. *Get involved.* Ask tough questions, then seek out the answers, or be willing to hold off on the answers. Get to know your professors. Make this a time to develop a Christian worldview and to build a foundation for the future. Take advantage of the advantages—professors who care, smaller classes, other Christians with whom you can develop lasting relationships, sharper minds, and warmer hearts.

2. *Be thankful.* Don't take your education for granted. There are many believers who would love to be at a school like yours but cannot afford it. If your parents have provided for this education, thank them.

3. *Get involved in ministry outside the campus.* A good school usually has a list of ministry opportunities, but you'll have to seek them out. My ministry to youth began when a Christian education professor on our campus told me about a church looking for a youth director. And there are great possibilities outside the campus and church as well. Check them out.

4. *Don't run away from the world.* Keep in touch with non-Christians. Don't spend all your time on   campus. Get involved in an organization or an activity away from the campus that involves non-Christians—a special interest group, a political party, a hiking club, or an aerobics class. Getting off campus into different groups of people will help you to widen your worldview and prevent you from isolating yourself.

To sum it all up, you should maximize the advantages and minimize the disadvantages of attending a Christian college. Brent Plate did, and he concluded, "My first year at a Christian school has been a great one. At this point in my life it has been perfect for me both spiritually and mentally. After having spent a couple of years in a secular college, I have really been able to see the many advantages of a Christian school."

CHAPTER

15

DON'T WAIT:
Making a Difference Now

Let me tell you about three friends of mine, all students. Kara Hallock is a sorority girl. Two summers ago, she applied to our World Deputation program and was assigned to a team in Northern Ireland. For a summer, she ministered to Irish kids, telling them about Christ and loving them unconditionally. It was a demanding summer in a land torn by strife, but she returned to school in the fall refreshed and renewed. Several months later, she became a volunteer with New Horizons, a ministry to kids on Seattle's streets. Street kids are a long way from sorority sisters. But that hasn't phased Kara—she's making a difference and she loves it. And her college career continues to prosper. She's pursuing her major, is well liked by her peers, and is active in her fellowship group.

Sean Shannon, a political science major, graduated from the University of Washington in 1987. During his junior and senior years, he invested ten to twelve hours a week as a Young Life leader at a high school club twenty-five minutes from campus. He did some weekend retreats and spent a week each summer with his guys at a Young Life camp. He made a difference at that high school and still enjoyed his college experience.

Eric Lingren is a "have desire...will travel" kind of guy. Whenever a mission opportunity comes up, he hits the road. He has served in Guatemala, the Philippines, Northern Ireland, and Bolivia. He has also been involved locally. Last year he got a group of fellow students together to go weekly to the children's hospital to work with psychologically disturbed kids. The presence of college students who cared made a difference in that hospital.

College is a place where it's easy to become *self-centered*. You think of *my* classes, *my* major, *my* roommate, *my* house, *my* friends, *my* future, *my* career. In college, your family is away and you're probably not married. So you can focus on yourself.

College is also a place where it's easy to become *campus centered*. That's natural. Your world revolves around the university, and so it's easy to become campus centered.

But I'd like to encourage you in this chapter to move beyond yourself and your campus and make a difference in the world *now*, not later. Right now, in college, you can have the kind of positive influence on lives that my three friends Kara, Sean, and Eric have had.

For years I have been telling students to make a difference *now*. In our ministry, we constantly try to encourage, equip, and deploy students. We'd like each student to have a cross-cultural experience before graduating. By cross cultural, I mean ministering to and with someone who doesn't fit into the college culture or the parental and high-school culture from which you came. These experiences can be done locally or internationally. They can be ongoing or very short term. We have some students who are teaching English each week to refugees from Cambodia. That's local and ongoing. But we also send out teams all over the United States and the world for one-week, two-week, three-month, and one-year ministries.

I also encourage students to make a difference in a non-cross-cultural way during the academic year and in the summers. Being part of the Big Brothers program fits into that category. Helping with a Young Life club at a nearby high school like Sean Shannon did is an example. Volunteering on a psych ward at a children's hospital as Eric did is another.

There are many ways to serve. In the last few years, our students have been involved in making a difference in the world. Here is a list of some of the things they have been doing:

o *Playing basketball for Sports Ambassadors in Latin America*

o *Volunteering as Big Brothers and Big Sisters*

o *Directing huddle groups at Fellowship of Christian Athletes camps.*

o *Building homes with Habitat for Humanity in Seattle, South Carolina, and Africa*

o *Being part of an evangelistic team that showed the film "Jesus" in Mexico and Guatamela*

o *Signing (doing sign language) for church services*

o *Teaching English to refugees*

o *Being part of a buddy system with international students*

o *Directing the youth program at other churches and serving on the volunteer staff with our church's youth program.*

o *Leading Young Life clubs*

o *Serving with New Horizon Ministries, which reaches out to street kids*

o *Putting together a Christian rap group and performing around the city*

o *Tutoring in foreign languages*

o *Ministering in summer programs in Scotland,*

Ireland, British Columbia, Philadelphia,
Mississippi, Los Angeles, India, Ghana, Nigeria,
the Philippines, Austria, Holland, and
Colombia
o *Sharing Christ in Eastern Europe*
o *Serving as camp counselors for Christian summer*
camps
o *Working with the handicapped*
o *Volunteering as aides in hospitals*
o *Teaching Sunday school*
o *Serving on the Haiti Medical Team*
o *Working at the Food Bank*

The list could go on and on. I'm sure you see the possibilities. But in the midst of the possibilities, several questions emerge. Why should I get involved? How will this involvement impact my experience at the university? Will it enhance or detract from my grades and extracurricular activities? And, if I decide to make a difference, how do I get involved? These are very legitimate questions.

Let's look at those questions individually.

Why should I get involved?

1. *There's a need in your community and the world.* People need to hear about Jesus. In "Stepping Out," a booklet designed as a guide for short-term missions, Douglas Millham says, "Two-thirds of the world is still waiting to hear the Gospel, and most of them don't yet have any way out of the frightful darkness of poverty and injustice that refuses to go away." Kids from one-parent families need a big brother or sister in their lives. Refugees need to learn English. Psych wards need volunteers. Needs abound, and we as Christians can't ignore those needs.

2. *God loves to use students.* In 1549, Francis Xavier said, "Tell the students to give up their small ambitions and come eastward to preach the gospel of Christ." Today, the call to spread the Gospel is still there. At this stage of your life, because you have minimal outside demands and maximum energy and enthusiasm, you can be part of a network of students making a significant difference. Recently Tony Campolo challenged a group of Harvard MBA students. He said to them, "Anybody can get a great job at IBM and be a success. But how many of you can go to Haiti and start a cooperative bakery among the poor?" That summer, half a dozen students did just as he suggested. Their lives were changed and so were the lives of some Haitian people.

3. *Be part of a winning team.* God is on the move. Every day 1,600 new churches begin and the Christian movement grows by 78,000 people. In 1987 nearly 60,000 North Americans were involved in short-term missionary service. That's ten times the number of people that were involved in 1977. Each year, God's mission team grows. God is developing a short-term mission movement that can encourage, enable, and assist the local church. Be a part of that team.

4. *It's good for you.* I always hated this explanation when my mother tried to force medicine down me or make me go to some event that I didn't want to attend. But "it's good for you" is true when it comes to making a difference now. Let me give you a few "good-for-you's."

- You'll grow spiritually. Spiritual growth happens naturally when you serve. Not only will you see the evidence of Christ's life *in* you, but you will also see the difference he makes *through* you.

- You'll get to discover and use your gifts and talents. And many of those talents will relate to your major. If you're in the school of nursing, for example, get on a medical team. If you're an engineering student, be part of a ministry that works to bring water to thirsty lands through irrigation.

- You'll grow personally as you meet people from different cultures and face demanding situations.

- You'll probably travel.

- You'll have something to look forward to when you're bored in your classes. In the midst of the worst lecture you ever heard, you can say, "In two months, Mexico."

- You'll learn more about the world, and your interest in places where you've formerly served will be sharpened because you've been there. Laura Swain, an adventuresome nurse, began her "cross-cultural career" as a student who served at a small medical clinic in Baja, Mexico one weekend a month. That experience increased her interest in making a difference in the world. Since that time, she has taken short-term assignments in Somalia, Beirut, and Mexico. Now when she reads the newspapers and watches television news, she especially cares about those three regions of the world. Her global focus has been enlarged by serving Christ.

How will this experience impact my overall college experience?

Doug Early gives a good answer: "In my personal experience and in viewing others who did the same, I am convinced that volunteering, going abroad, or taking a quarter off school to serve enhances school and what you're doing there. Ministering to others allows you to be involved with people who aren't doing what you're doing and gives you a fresh perspective."

Doug continues, "And don't be afraid if you're initial interest in serving is partially selfish, i.e., it will look good on your resume, people you've admired have done that and you want to look good too, and so forth. God uses everything. I can almost guarantee that once you're involved you'll soon realize that you *need* to do it or you *want* to do it *for others*. What more could you want to learn during your time at school?"

These are words from a guy who volunteered to go to China to teach English for a year and who faced a great deal of pain and hardship because of his health. Service wasn't easy for Doug, but he came back recommending it and feeling that he'd like to go again.

Ministry and mission may not be listed in your college catalog, but they are the best way to add to your education. Author Joe Bayly used to say, "Don't let school interfere with your child's education." I say, "Don't let college interfere with yours." One of the best ways you can educate yourself and broaden your "curriculum" is to make a difference in the world.

How do I get involved?

1. *Look around where you are.* What's going on where you live? What ministries exist near your campus? Is there a ministry to high school students in the community? Is there a ministry to refugees or street kids? Is there a church or ministry in the area that sends out teams in the summer? Ask them how to get involved.

2. *Write or make a phone call.* If you can't get involved nearby, or if you want to learn about some other ministries, contact organizations like these:

• Intercristo's Christian Placement Service. Call toll free 1-800-426-1342 or write Intercristo, 19303 Fremont Ave., N. Seattle, WA 98133. They can provide you with a list of opportunities that match your interests and skills.

• Evangelical Foreign Missions Associations, P.O. Box 395, Wheaton, IL 60819-0395. They can help you in much the same way that Intercristo can.

• If you're interested in construction, contact Habitat for Humanity, Americus, GA 31709. Their phone number is 912-924-6935.

• If you want to use your athletic abilities in a missions project, contact Sports Ambassadors at 55 Fair Drive, Costa Mesa, CA.

• For summer evangelistic opportunities, write Campus Crusade, Dept. 36-50, Arrowhead Springs, CA. 92414.

3. *Act on your information.*

In the course of a four-year education, you will have four Christmas breaks, four spring breaks, and at least three summer vacations. Set aside at least a couple of these breaks for short-term service. If time permits, get involved in a ministry during the year. And remember—it's better to light a candle than to curse the darkness. Your time might seem too limited to make a difference, the world might seem too dark to penetrate, but light the candle, watch others light theirs, and trust God with the results.

CHAPTER

16

A FEW LAST WORDS:
Wrapping it Up

For fifteen chapters, we've been discussing how to survive college. We've looked at discoveries, choices, spiritual survival, developing a Christian worldview, time management, how to study, where to live and how to get along, handling pressures, surviving failure, maximizing the Christian college experience, and making a difference in the world. You've absorbed a lot of information by now, and maybe you're feeling a bit overwhelmed.

To help you deal with information overload, any good professor will provide a summary for you at the end of his or her lecture. Although I hope this book has not seemed like a lecture as much as a guided discussion, I'd like to do what we'd expect a professor to do: summarize.

If this were the only chapter you were going to read (and some of you may have skipped to this chapter), what could I say that would wrap it all up?

I decided not to say much at all.

Instead, I've determined to let those who contributed to the book have the last word. Twenty-three people, mostly men and women still in college or recently graduated, helped me write this book by contributing to a specific chapter where they had expertise. In this chapter, I've asked them to give me a one or two sentence "key idea" on the secret of how to survive college. I have tried to group their answers somewhat in a logical sequence.

Here are their specific thoughts, complete with short biographical sketches and photos. I hope you will enjoy hearing what they have to say.

On Not Letting School Interfere with Your College Education

"Students were not created for school; school was created for students. Hang on to the proper perspective."

Jim Allen graduated in 1987 from the University of Washington with a degree in psychology. He was a member of Beta Theta Pi fraternity. After spending a year serving as a missionary in Africa, he is now on staff as an intern at University Presbyterian Church in Seattle.

"Finding a balance between studying and social life is essential. College is for getting an education not only in academics, but also in life."

Kim Ebeling graduated from the University of Washington with a B.S. in psychology in 1988. She was a member of Delta Delta Delta sorority. She has been involved in short-term missions to both Latin America and India. Like Jim Allen, she is currently an intern with University Ministries at University Presbyterian Church in Seattle.

"College is like a laboratory experiment: You are put into all kinds of situations and environments, and the lessons learned will be valuable for the rest of your life. Therefore, try new things, get involved, and do your best in everything. You'll find these experiments will probably equip you better for life than the classroom education."

Rod Handley serves as the Assistant State Director

for the Fellowship of Christian Athletes in Washington State as well as the Ministry Coordinator for college students at University Presbyterian Church in Seattle. He graduated from Central Washington University in 1982 with a degree in accounting and worked four years in the international accounting firm of Ernst and Whinney before going into full-time Christian ministry. He also is the chaplain for the Seattle Supersonics of the National Basketball Association and was an Academic All-American football player during college.

"Realize college is much more than a means to an end and that you are presently forming opinions and habits that will likely remain with you the rest of your life. Don't become so wrapped up in your goals and aspirations that you neglect to take advantage of the many valuable opportunities for learning, growth, and friendships that college has to offer."

Mark "Hogie" Hogendobler was raised in Virginia Beach, Virginia. A Phi Beta Kappa scholar, he graduated with highest honors from Princeton University with a degree in molecular biology in 1987. He served for a year as University Ministries Intern at University Presbyterian Church in Seattle and is presently on staff with Young Life at Mercer Island, Washington.

"Keep school work in perspective. It's important but it's not everything!"

Sue Harris graduated from the University of

Washington in 1988 with a B.A. in business administration and was active in her sorority, Kappa Kappa Gamma. She married Stu Harris in July of 1988. She is currently an intern at University Presbyterian Church.

On Relationships

"What is essential to survival? An accountability fellowship: a group of people who will help keep you

balanced, who won't let you make grades your god, and who won't let you get away with a ""free-for-all" mentality. That's what's needed in my estimation."

Mike Gaffney graduated from the University of Washington in 1987. He played for the Huskies in football for four years. Currently he is the Director of University Ministries at the First Presbyterian Church in Boulder, Colorado. He is married to Shari, an elementary school teacher.

"Build a support network of friends with whom you share similar beliefs. Questioning your beliefs will

be natural, but make sure you have some peers in whom to confide your struggles as well as your joys."

Dick Rant grew up in Boise, Idaho. In 1988 he received a Speech Communications degree from the University of Washington. He was Captain of the U.W. Tennis team and has been active in the Fellowship of Christian Athletes. Presently Dick serves as an intern with University Ministries.

"Take time to invest in relationships. It is far too easy to float through college knowing a lot of names and faces but never really building true friendships."

Pete Shimer graduated from the University of Washington in 1984 in accounting cum laude. He is an audit manager at the international firm of Touche Ross, where he has worked since graduation. He played basketball for four years at the U of W and was president of his fraternity.

"If you want to make a difference in the lives of other college students, make sure you hang out where you live. Don't be so involved in other activities or so anxious to move out to your own apartment that you don't spend time with the guys where you live. And if you want to learn to make a difference in the world, get involved in a short-term mission team. That experience will change your life."

Steve Call graduated with a B.A. in economics from the University of Washington in 1986. He was active in his fraternity (Theta Chi), served one year as an intern with University Ministries, and now is Missions Coordinator there, challenging and enabling students to be involved in short-term missions. He was married in the summer of 1986 to Lisa. He loves basketball and has played for Sports Ambas-

A Few Last Words

sadors the past two summers in Latin America.

"Choose your friends as you would compatriots in a monumental struggle for significance and joy and the freedom of righteousness, for you will face those very things together."

Patty Burgin graduated from Oregon State University in 1972 with majors in international relations, Spanish, and secondary education. She became involved with Campus Crusade for Christ while in college and upon graduation joined the Campus Crusade staff. She served from 1972-76 on the campus of UCLA before becoming a member of the National Leadership Team of Campus Crusade. A pioneer of ministries to professional and pre-professional people in both the United States and Eastern Europe, she is also one of the founding coordinators for the World-wide Student Network.

On School and Self

"Don't take yourself too seriously. Life gets even more complicated when you don't laugh enough.

Freedom to achieve comes from being able to enjoy yourself during the mistakes!"

Carolyn Duffy graduated from the University of Washington in 1985 with a B.A. in speech communications. She has enjoyed working the last few years in ministry to high school and college students.

"Don't feel like you have to declare your major right away. It's okay if you aren't sure what you like. Try out different subjects and enjoy yourself!"

Nancy Seifert graduated from the University of Washington with a B.A. in art and an elementary teaching certificate. She was active in her sorority (Pi Beta Phi), and she spent three of her college summers working with children in Canada and California. She is currently a sixth grade teacher in Edmonds, WA

"Establish a framework of real-life application upon which to hang academic concepts. And always check what you are learning against what you know from the 'real world.'"

Scott Burnett graduated from Nyack College (New York) in 1981 with a Bachelor of Music Composition degree. He studied systematic musicology at the University of Washington in 1984—85. After spending a year ministering with a contemporary Christian music group in the United States and Europe, he currently is a principal at Darkhorse Musicmedia Company, which produces video and film scores as well as records and tapes. Scott is married to Hilary and they have two children.

"God has called us to be faithful, not successful. So do that which God has placed before you. It's not usually the easy road, but it is the best. Like the Nike commercial says, 'Just do it'"

Eric Lingren graduated from Seattle Pacific

University in 1986 with a B.A. in chemistry and a B.S. in biology. He was an intern in University Ministries at University Presbyterian Church, Seattle, for one year and is currently preparing for a short-term mission assignment in Latin America.

"Take time to discover your gifts. Consider a major based on your gifts rather than choosing a major that is popular or a major that family and friends are pressuring you to enter."

Laura Swain graduated from Point Loma College in San Diego with a B.S. in nursing and has enjoyed a variety of experiences from nursing in the neonatal intensive care unit at the University of Washington Hospital to nursing in refugee camps in East Africa and doing emergency relief work in Beirut, Lebanon. Currently she divides her time between nursing and ministering to college students.

On God

"None of the knowledge taught at school is more important than one's personal knowledge of God."

Laurie Wheeler is a senior at the University of Washington who has a major in drama and a minor in English. She spent the last two years doing youth ministry, but in her senior year is concentrating on ministering within her sorority.

"It is essential to remember that although our collegiate quest for knowledge is important, our quest

for God must hold the highest place in our lives. Holding Christ as preeminent is the key to survival in all of life, college included."

Jim Francese is a graduate student at the University of Washington in chemical engineering. He graduated from Cornell University in 1986.

At Cornell, he was a member of Sigma Nu fraternity. He and his wife, Lisa, a graduate from Cornell in the field of nutrition, have been married for one year.

"I think Proverbs 3:5-6 are key verses for survival in college as well as in life. You need to focus on the

Lord to get through school. As soon as academics, athletics, or social functions become the focus, everything falls apart."

Brent Plate, a senior at Seattle Pacific University, is studying religion and philosophy. He eventually would like to teach on the college level and also spend time ministering in Europe.

"The true survivors in both college and life beyond are those who continually turn to God in success and failure, when life is easy and when it's tough, knowing that he is the only real judge of our worth and that he is in the business of turning ugly ducklings into beautiful swans."

Sue Jernberg graduated from the University of Washington in 1987 with a B.A. in speech pathology.

She is currently working on her master's degree in that field and at the same time serving on the University Ministries staff as an intern at University Presbyterian Church. She has been involved in a variety of mission experiences in Latin America.

"While in college, work with God to develop a vision. Try many things, but eventually focus your interests and commitments into a unified vision for how you and God will use your life to impact the world. Plan. Set long- and short-term goals and commit all of your plans and goals to the Lord. While

enjoying your time in college, delight yourself in the Lord and welcome him into every corner of your life, trusting him there. Do this and he will give you the desires of your heart."

Mark Preslar graduated magna cum laude from Arizona State University in 1982 with majors in Russian and Spanish. He received his M.A. in Russian language and Soviet studies from the University of Arizona in 1984. He has studied at both Leningrad State University and Moscow State University in Russia. He is currently completing his doctorate in Slavic linguistics at the University of Washington and has five years teaching experience on the university level. Mark also has extensive missions experience in Latin America and Europe.

On Not Finishing College

"My life has been a spiritual quest. I remember praying for 'wisdom and knowledge' when I was just a kid. I thought that quest would take me through college since a college degree was one of my heart's desires. However, marriage and family were also my heart's desires, and the latter was the path I chose. I have not been sorry for my choice, although I wasted a lot of emotional energy and time because I felt I'd failed by not completing college and I dealt with a great deal of guilt. But I realized that if you don't 'survive college,' God still has other options for you. He can and does redeem our shortcomings. Trust in him, seek his ways and his Word, lean not on your own understanding and he will make your paths straight. We can fill our

hearts and minds with so many facts and not leave room for the person of Jesus, who is Truth eternally."

Jo Anne Wood was born and raised in rural Kansas. She married her childhood sweetheart, Ardean Wood, in 1950, and they raised two sons. She attended college for two years. In addition to being a wife and mother, she worked for fourteen years at Edmonds Community college and has served as Administrative Assistant to Denny and Marilyn Rydberg at University Presbyterian Church the last four years.

On the Opportunity of College

"Go for it. You only live once."
Doug Early graduated from the University of Washington with a B.A. in English literature. He spent a year in China teaching English and is currently pursuing his master's degree in theology at Regent College in Vancouver, British Columbia.

One Final Word

"If you want to survive college, read the whole book, not just this chapter."

Denny Rydberg graduated from Seattle Pacific University in 1967 with a B.A. in psychology. He did graduate work at Western Washington University. He has served as a youth director, Christian education director, magazine editor, company vice president, director of operations and consultant for a film company, and now he is Director of University Ministries with his wife, Marilyn, at University Presbyterian Church in Seattle. Denny and Marilyn have four children: Heather, Joshua, Jeremy, and Jonathan.